OMNIBUS PRESS
London/New York
Paris/Sydney/Copenhagen
Berlin/Madrid/Tokyo

Mark Paytress

Copyright © 2004 Omnibus Press
(A Division of Music Sales Limited)

Cover and book designed by Chloë Alexander
Picture research by Sarah Bacon

ISBN: 0.7119.9887.6
Order Number: OP49544

Exclusive Distributors
Music Sales Limited,
8/9 Frith Street,
London W1D 3JB, UK.

Music Sales Corporation,
257 Park Avenue South,
New York, NY 10010, USA.

Macmillan Distribution Services,
53 Park West Drive,
Derrimut, Vic 3030,
Australia.

To the Music Trade only:
Music Sales Limited,
8/9 Frith Street,
London W1D 3JB, UK.

Every effort has been made to trace the copyright
holders of the photographs in this book but one or
two were unreachable. We would be grateful if the
photographers concerned would contact us.

Printed by: Cox & Wyman Ltd, Reading, Berks.

A catalogue record for this book is available from the
British Library.

Visit Omnibus Press on the web at
www.omnibuspress.com

Contents

INTRODUCTION

KURT COBAIN MIGHT HAVE BEEN MOTIVATED BY CONTRADICTORY DRIVES, BUT one thing is certain: he did not want to become Elvis Presley, a rebel who'd rocked the mid-Fifties but who later roly-poly'd into star-spangled orthodoxy. Yet there was much to unite these two icons of American rock-'n'roll. Their backwater origins were remarkably similar – both were boys from nowhere with fantasies of transcending the low-life that had been mapped out for them. And so, in a way, were their destinies.

Sandwiched between them was thirty years of rock history and a salutary lesson in tarnished innocence. Presley was a raw and impressionable talent who sang to please his mother, patented a rock'n'roll attitude he once famously encapsulated with the words, "gone, real gone", and ended up serenading the well-heeled at mealtimes. Presley's fate provided a template for rock's tendency to disappoint, and Kurt Cobain had no desire to repeat the mistake.

Elvis once embodied the hopes of an emerging generation of teenagers, and the fears of their despairing elders. His lip-curlin', hip-swivelin', hick-celebrating antics had conspired to create the Twentieth century's most controversial anti-hero, though he had become such a thing largely by chance. Sure, he was oddly distinctive, but it was young America's subconscious desire for an Elvis (having road-tested James Dean and Marlon Brando) that transformed this Mississippi truck driver into the epitome of everything wild and indecent about subterranean Yankee culture.

Within months, Presley had been rendered harmless: Hollywood, the US Army, and a whole lot more Hollywood followed. His untamed abandon had been controlled, commodified. Suitably neutered, Presley ended up doing the establishment's policing for them, infamously advising the White House of the immoral and improper of those among rock's next generation of 'goners'.

There was an oft overlooked irony here, though. With barely an anti-establishment bone in his entire body, Presley still managed to lose control. It wasn't just the drugs – prescription ones of course, but no less mind-altering or mood-changing than those gobbled up by the free radicals of the post-psychedelic world. Life in Elvisville, in his Graceland mansion, was Little, Lynchian America writ large. Televisions weren't just there to be watched; they were there to be shot to pieces. Burgers weren't bought from the local drive-in; they'd be flown in from the other side of the country, and not just one but dozens of them. Elvis sought to make peace with his maker, but at the same time, was destined to self-destruct, his ever swelling body increasingly dependent on Dr. Nick's mind-bending palliatives.

Elvis was more "real gone" at the end of his life than he was at its outset, though Kurt Cobain wouldn't have seen it that way. The genuine madness of life on the inside lane of American white-bread culture sits awkwardly alongside the romantic tradition of the rock outsider – in which Cobain invested so heartily. Elvis had rejected it almost as soon as he realised he was part of it. Instead, the germ he unwittingly unleashed was carried down the decades by a long line of beautifully formed young corpses – and Rolling Stone Keith Richards. But by the time Cobain raised his dreamily disobedient head above the parapet of a simple life, the Romantic Rock Star had long descended into caricature.

The cynic in Kurt Cobain suspected that it was nine-tenths bullshit anyway. The idealist in him couldn't help buying into it. And just as Elvis's acquiescence grew ever more absurd the older he got, Cobain's estrangement from the rest of the world magnified under the spotlight of fame. He wasn't going to make the same mistake. Cobain fought desperately against homogenisation, against becoming just another rock star from humble beginnings who'd got rich on the emotional uncertainties of his generation, against the very idea that comfort in life could be cheaply purchased.

Neither Presley (modern America's Minister of Culture) or Cobain (its conscience) were equipped to deal particularly well with goldfish-bowl stardom. In their bid to take control over *something*, as their lives span out into all directions, both turned inwards, their bodies becoming virtual battlegrounds. Presley's boomed and busted, usually depending on whether a tour was imminent or not. Cobain, instinctively attracted to heroin's protecting veil, was soon playing cat-and-mouse with his addiction, a reflection of the do-or-die tendency so apparent in his contradictory personality. When even that failed, only the loaded shotgun would do, rather than the long-haul to self-repair that would – he assumed – necessitate the surrender of the creative urges that gave him a reason for living.

When Kurt Cobain flogged his record collection so that he could travel the 100 miles or so up to Seattle to see Black Flag (California's leading hardcore punk band), the last thing on his mind was Elvis Presley. It was August 1984, and in his eyes, the disobedient tradition 'The King' had set in motion forty years earlier was marching authoritatively on. For Cobain – despite a nasty experience with The Clash's *Sandinista!* – that meant punk rock.

In America, where one musical trend doesn't necessarily negate a previous one, punk peaceably co-existed alongside classic heavy rock. Cobain later understood the ideological antipathy of the two genres, but by the mid-Eighties, when he'd started writing and recording with his own band, an unholy fusion was already taking place. That was thanks to a new breed of fiercely independent, hybrid American bands – Sonic Youth, Butthole Surfers, Big Black, Killdozer, Scratch Acid, Flipper and Hüsker Dü.

Punk's outsider status appealed to Cobain on an emotional level. Unlike metal, a mainstream cultural currency even among those who didn't really care about music, punk appeared to fit the one-man rebellion he'd been waging ever since he'd begun to think for himself. Punks were articulate. They reflected society's horror and ugliness back at itself. Sometimes, those types that Cobain derided as "moron dudes" called them as faggots. These were the "gone" guys, adrift from society. But by the mid-Eighties, with the self-preservation-obsessed 'Straight Edge' movement dominating the American punk scene, it was the metal guys who were literally out of their heads.

The meeting of those two subcultures presented Cobain with a dilemma. Metal fans expected large helpings of showmanship – stage-diving, the ritual sacrifice of instruments – alongside mind-crunching riffs rattled out at high volume. Punk idealists, or at least their inheritors, wanted to hear critique – the truth, the pain behind the noise. For a while, he managed to unite both, enjoying an unexpected level of success in the process. But as the shock of Nirvana's whirlwind emergence mutated into familiarity, the weight of responsibility began to pile up, both to his public and his own conscience. Where next for the rich, feted rebel?

From the moment Nirvana broke internationally, late in 1990, until his suicide in April 1994, Kurt Cobain struggled to reconcile the contradictions that served to pull him apart. To most commentators, Nirvana was a loser/slacker band, the epitome of the estranged, Reaganised-into-submission Generation X. And yet rock had rarely sounded so alive, so potent in years.

There were other contradictory elements at play: masculine/feminine, public/private, pop/punk, violence/non-violence, celebrity/anonymity, straight/'gone'. The band embodied this discord in its music, the classic Nirvana sound a clash of soft and hard, quiet and loud, and nowhere bettered than on songs such as 'Smells Like Teen Spirit' and 'Come As You Are'. Conflict was at the heart of Cobain's *oeuvre*, something he revealed when he tried to play down the meaning in his songs to band biographer Michael Azerrad. "They are all basically saying the same things," he said. "I have this conflict between good and evil, and man and woman, and that's about it."

Try as he might, Presley couldn't hide the helplessness that was written all over his body. But Cobain had no wish to hide his. As a nemesis of sorts to Presleyian orderliness, he was compelled to lay bare the sores that fester beneath shiny, happy PLC America. He knew too that he was implicated in the entire charade, a burden that became more troublesome as Nirvana's fame spread. And, in his private moments, Cobain remained adamant that he wouldn't concede control without a fight. He would never do a Presley, and succumb to a fatal dose of courtier-smothered complacency. That would have been too easy, too predictable. Cobain wanted the satisfaction of knowing that he'd orchestrated every aspect of his own deliberate exit.

Bleach

Tupelo TUP CD6, August 1989; UK release Sub Pop SP 34

Reissued by Geffen as GEF 24433 in April 1992
with additional tracks 'Big Cheese' and 'Downer'

BEFORE GLIMPSES OF THE ADULT WORLD CHANGED HIS PERSPECTIVE COMPLETELY, Kurt Cobain's musical upbringing was unexceptional. He was raised on The Beatles and Monkees hits favoured by his father, then hit his teens to the sounds of AOR stalwarts such as Queen, ELO, Meatloaf and The Cars.

By the time he was 14, in 1981, Cobain was aware of punk rock, though preferred to play standards such as Led Zeppelin's 'Stairway To Heaven' and The Cars' 'My Best Friend's Girl' on his newly-acquired guitar. Three years later, 'the conversion' took place. He'd befriended Aberdeen's only hardcore band, The Melvins, eagerly watched them rehearse and sometimes acted as the band's roadie. The band's front-man Buzz Osborne made up listening cassettes to enhance Cobain's education; another band member, Matt Lukin, took him to see his first show, Black Flag, in Seattle. Kurt sold most of his record collection to fund the trip.

His first involvement with a genuine rock band (The Melvins issued two albums during the mid-Eighties while Cobain was around) certainly left its mark. Much of *Bleach*, Nirvana's debut album, sounds like a re-run of The Melvins' grunge-defining *10 Songs* LP, issued three years earlier, in 1986. That's probably one good reason why it wasn't singled out for special treatment by the band's record label, Sub Pop, who at this early stage suspected there was more mileage in Mudhoney and Tad.

Punk and metal had been mutual bedfellows in the States for much of the decade, invigorating a scene that had started out rather like a poor interpretation of third generation British punk. Before long, a peculiarly American muscularity began to creep into the sound, from Los Angeles' Black Flag to Chicago's Big Black. Though separated by geography and time, both were marked by a strong work ethic, a sense of discipline that had little relevance to the bands emanating from the Pacific North-West later in the decade. Instead, the more ramshackle, druggy element that helped characterise grunge (and gave rise to the loser/slacker tags), had been forged by more dissident musical souls like New York's Sonic Youth and the Texas-based Butthole Surfers.

For the time being, Nirvana eschewed the neo-psychedelia of those bands, sticking closely to The Melvins' template of dense, metal-derived riffs with the spontaneous, despairing attitude of punk. Between the mid-Eighties and 1989, when sessions for *Bleach* were completed, Cobain's musical referents changed slowly. A false start as The Sell-Outs, a Creedence

Clearwater Revival covers band (featuring Cobain on drums and Chris Novoselic on guitar and vocals), soon gave way to the pre-Nirvana Skid Row early in 1987. With Cobain now on guitar and vocals, Novoselic on bass and drummer Aaron Burckhard, the group was already touting a set crammed with future Nirvana songs. More than that, Cobain's lazy vocal drawl was already giving the group its distinctive edge.

The group's route to Seattle, Sub Pop Records and *Bleach* received a significant boost when the trio uprooted to Olympia. The capital of Washington State, Olympia, was smaller than Seattle, but boasted its own alternative radio station and thriving alternative music scene. After the cultural desert that was Aberdeen, Olympia seemed like an artistic oasis, and Cobain flourished in his new surroundings, painting, writing songs and finding sympathetic ears for his music. By the time Nirvana recorded their first proper demo, at Reciprocal Studios, Seattle, on January 23, 1988, drummer Burckhard had gone, and their old Melvins pal Dale Crover (who had already recorded seven home demos with Cobain back in autumn 1986) sat in for the session. The trio taped ten songs in six hours; the bill came to just $152.44; and producer Jack Endino was impressed enough to pass a copy on to Bruce Pavitt.

Pavitt had launched his independent label Sub Pop in July 1986 with the *Sub Pop 100* compilation, a various artists collection from the America-wide underground. Alongside contributions by Sonic Youth, Scratch Acid and The Wipers were two local acts: Steve Fisk and the U-Men. When Jonathan Poneman came on board, providing additional cash, the label began to concentrate on talent from the local scene: Green River, Soundgarden, Mudhoney and Tad. After hearing the Endino tape, Pavitt and Poneman added Nirvana to Sub Pop's growing roster. The group was still a trio, though by now, the temping Dale Crover had been replaced by drummer Chad Channing, who brought with him an enthusiasm for hard-hitting late Sixties spoilers Vanilla Fudge and the obligatory Aerosmith. With a committed line-up now in place, Nirvana launched themselves with 'Love Buzz' single, which soon sold out the 1,000 copies pressed as part of Sub Pop's subscription-only Singles Club. Suitably encouraged, they returned to Reciprocal Studios over the 1988-89 New Year period to record what became the band's debut album.

It was a typically low-budget affair, with five tracks taped on Endino's eight-track machine on December 24, and a further five on December 29, with finishing touches added on January 24. The deal with Sub Pop was sufficiently loose that the band financed the sessions themselves. Acquiring a fourth member, ex-Soundgarden guitarist Jason Everman, who stumped up the full $606.17, helped immeasurably. It wasn't even a case of pay-to-play: despite his credit on the sleeve, Everman didn't contribute a note, and barely six months later, he was out. The recruitment of a second guitarist suggested that Cobain was looking for more flexibility in the band's sound, but before that could be fully considered, there was the business of making a tape of the bands original set – which is largely what *Bleach* was. In that respect, Everman was surplus to requirements. Cobain rarely bothered to add guitar overdubs during the recording, and when he did, he knew exactly what he wanted. The last thing Nirvana needed was a second guitarist.

The sound of *Bleach* was raw and uncompromising, and this was suitably reflected in its basic black-and-white sleeve, depicting the hirsute four-piece in the monochromatic rush of live performance. In keeping with the penny-pinching budget, the photographer Tracy Marander (then Cobain's partner) wasn't paid. Goodwill no doubt got her through, plus the satisfaction that her shot was important in shaping the wider public's perception of Nirvana. Unsurprisingly, it wasn't that far removed to the 'Blue Cheer for the Nineties' aura that was already beginning to crystallise around Mudhoney.

Nirvana's early live shows were closer to edgy, punk rock affairs than they ever were to showy and testosterone-induced hard rock. This wasn't always reflected on the *Bleach* debut album, which was a more uptight brand of dirge-rock. Its sound could be traced all the way back, via The Melvins, through to the oppressive doom-riffs of Black Sabbath, and further still, to the claustrophobic heavy metal psychedelia of Blue Cheer. One possible punk rock reference was Cobain's decision to restyle himself 'Kurdt Kobain', though even this smacked as much of metallic 'K-K-Kerrang!' stylistic excess as it did of the self-obliterating tendencies that once compelled punks to deny their names. (He later maintained, unconvincingly, that the alternative spelling was the result of a chance mistake.) In a band biography circulated just prior to the album's release, Cobain offered a few pointers to journalists struggling for reference points. "Nirvana," he suggested, "sounds like Black Sabbath – playing The Knack, Black Flag, Led Zeppelin and The Stooges, with a pinch of The Bay City Rollers." That eclectic concoction was better suited as a description of what was to come: for the time being, Nirvana's songs were – with one notable exception – considerably more one-dimensional than that list suggested.

Sub Pop's own description, printed in its summer 1989 catalogue, was vague but closer to the mark. *Bleach* was described as "hypnotic and righteous heaviness from these Olympia pop stars". Some bright spark, obviously overdosing on hyperbole, added: "They're young, they've got their own van and they're going to make us rich!" Reasonably impressive though it was, *Bleach* was hardly another *Rumours* or *Brothers In Arms* just waiting to get the entire US of A humming along. It was an album made strictly for underground consumption, for the kind of people who'd get a kick out of wearing the new Nirvana publicity T-shirt that bore the legend, "Cracksmokin' satan-worshipin' fudge-packin' motherfucks".

With the tape in the bag, Nirvana became one of several Seattle bands who ventured beyond the Washington borders to play some shows in California in February 1989. While there, the band and their Sup Pop protectors Pavitt and Poneman kept seeing "Bleach Your Works" posters displayed everywhere, as part of a campaign to slow the spread of Aids through the drug-using community. If choosing *Bleach* as an album title was a personal in-joke with its own drug connections (and grunge, like most rock subcultures, went hand-in-hand with dope of some kind or another), it also worked on other levels, implying colourlessness, emotional fatigue, or even chemically-enhanced purity. All were probably appropriate. At the end of January 1989, the four-piece Nirvana returned to Reciprocal to record what Cobain later described as four "weird, quirky songs", with the intention of including them on *Bleach*. None of these, the Vaselines-influenced 'Beans', 'Money Will Roll Right In', 'Run Rabbit Run' and 'The Eagle Has Landed', has since emerged, which perhaps bears out Jonathan Poneman's assessment: he hated them. Had this kooky quartet been included, perhaps Cobain's later jaundiced view of the album might have been tempered. Within months of its release, he was already distancing himself from the record, describing the band's approach to it as similar to the way they'd record a radio session. "I hate *Bleach* so much now," he said months after its release. That comment probably says as much about Cobain's attitude to his work – and perhaps his life – as it does about the record.

Clearly, the songwriting on the album is not on a par with his later work. The production is simple and effective, but largely without frills. Cobain's major strength, his voice, struggles to be heard amid the detuned instruments and the ceaseless rhythms. But *Bleach* didn't – and doesn't – deserve such a lambasting. What irked Cobain most about the record was its small-mindedness, its limited ambition. It had been tailored towards a small but eager alternative audience. It was recorded in great haste, and with little expense, with the band congratulating themselves that great rock was supposed to be done that way.

More than that, *Bleach* was a fan's eye view of rock'n'roll, conceived and executed with an innocence that would soon be shattered. By 1990, Cobain had seen enough of the business to realise that the recording process is only one of several steps necessary in order for a record to become "great". With this knowledge came money and power, and disturbing feelings of premeditation and detachment that Cobain would struggle with for the rest of his life. The irony inherent in the band's name – a release into a blissful state – was only just becoming apparent.

BLEW

(Note: all songs written by Kurt Cobain otherwise stated.)

COBAIN, never a wordy songwriter even though he had plenty to rail about, kept the lyrics to a bare minimum throughout *Bleach*, most songs consisting merely of one verse and chorus repeated to suit the song's length. Often he would insist that his words were barely worth scrutinising, especially during the early years: their main purpose was simply to give him something to sing. Meanings, if any could be ascertained from such Spartan evidence, were as likely to operate on a subconscious level as a literal one, given that most were hastily written to order, often just prior to the recording sessions. You don't have to be a believer in the power of the Surrealists' technique of automatic writing to subscribe to the idea that something written in haste can say at least as much as something that is worthy and over laboured. It's worth pointing out, then, that *Bleach* opens with the phrase, "If you wouldn't mind...". Without wishing to spoil the surprise, Cobain's final song (proper) on a Nirvana studio album also ends in a similarly apologetic manner.

His words generally avoided the conceited style favoured by many lyricists who can't help but let it be known that they have something important to say. Instead, the varying shades of disappointment that ran through Cobain's work were delivered in a lackadaisical style that others would have shunned. You couldn't ascertain much from the handful of phrases that made up 'Blew', but with words like "lose", "leave", "stain", "strain" and "shame" providing the punchlines, a certain down-at-mouth philosophy seemed to prevail. (Not to mention 'Blew' as a variant of 'blue', as in feeling blue/miserable.) Almost always as important, though, is the manner in which the lyrics are delivered. This provides the crux of the Nirvana point of view, with Cobain vacillating between casual nonchalance and downright indignation, a simple juxtaposition that provided the band with its defining leitmotif.

This sense of laid-back loser chic was emphasised by a dramatic de-tuning of the guitars, two full notes lower than is usual in rock. That gave the song its gruff, malcontented mood, a feeling introduced right at the start with Novoselic's bass doing the musical equivalent of a rusty old Harley revving itself back into shape. As Cobain's vocal line mirrored the riff, the overall effect was of a Reagan-era response to Steppenwolf's 'Born To Be Wild': check out the final, unconvincing exhortation that "you could do anything" (note: 'could' not 'can').

Outside Seattle, 'Blew' was probably most indie enthusiasts introduction to Nirvana. Not only did it kick off *Bleach*, it also became the band's first UK single, the lead track on a 12" that coupled it with the debut 45, 'Love Buzz', plus two previously unreleased songs, 'Been A Son' and 'Stain'.

FLOYD THE BARBER

Two SONGS on *Bleach* had been rescued from the original Reciprocal session, taped almost a year before the rest of the album. Whether this is due to drummer Dale Crover's hard-hitting efforts, or simply because the feel of the re-recorded version with Chad Channing wasn't up to it, is unclear. Certainly the savagery with which the trio attacks this, one of the band's earliest songs, is equalled by Cobain's vocal, which by all accounts he recorded while lying inebriated on the floor. Despite the fact that the earlier, preferred performance had to be remixed, it still sounded muddy, if impressively Melvins-like. Even the ending seemed to peter out unexpectedly, which was surprising, given that the song had been part of the Nirvana set list since early 1987, when the band was still playing a version of Cher's 'Gypsies, Tramps And Thieves' (sung, no doubt hilariously badly, by Chris Novoselic).

'Floyd The Barber' was originally a character from the sanitised world of *The Andy Griffith Show*, a popular Sixties sitcom which portrayed small-town American life in such a cosy fashion that the actors must have endured great difficulty in keeping their apple pie down. Cobain once told his cousin that the programme represented "exactly the world I'm running away from": no surprise, then, to learn that the song's main character is tied up, assaulted and eventually murdered in full view of other characters from the show, Obie and Aunt Bea. It pretty much summed up Cobain's attitude to life back in Aberdeen, perfumed by the scent of small-town suffocation.

ABOUT A GIRL

The MELANCHOLIC E minor to G chord change has been used with great effect many times before, not least by T. Rex mainman Marc Bolan. In this instance, it provided a dramatic respite from the onslaught of restless guitar riffing, flailing rhythms and sandpaper vocals, earning 'About A Girl' the accolade of being Nirvana's first proper 'pop' song. ('Polly', another track that didn't sit easily on the band's punk/HM interface, was written around the same time, in the immediate pre-*Bleach* period.)

'About A Girl' was an early Nirvana rarity in another respect: it was written to order in response to a request by Cobain's then live-in partner Tracy Marander, with whom he'd been sharing a flat in Olympia since autumn 1987. The musical tenderness, emphasised by the absence of any abrasive effects like fuzz or distortion on the main guitar figure, was undercut by Cobain's caustic lyric, which seemed to delight in his manipulative attitude towards the relationship. Unsurprisingly, the affair ended in early summer 1990 when Marander moved out.

Cobain later suggested that putting the song on *Bleach* was "a risk", in that its avowedly pop values would have offended alternative rock purists. Perhaps so, but alternative rock in the States was inextricably bound up with college-rock supremos R.E.M., and rejoicing in melody seemed to be no bar to contra-rock kudos.

'About A Girl' was one of the few songs from *Bleach* that Nirvana took with them into the Nineties: a live version turned up on the 'Sliver' single, and the track was chosen to open the band's memorable *Unplugged* appearance.

SCHOOL

MANY OF Nirvana's earliest songs began with howls of feedback. This was usually because the amplifiers and effects pedals were cranked up so high that it was unavoidable, but it also became an integral part of the music, adding to the sense of drama and the mood of sensory overload. On 'School', the introductory whine of feedback rises until Cobain enters with a simple buzzsaw riff, propelling the song into one of the band's most successful exercises in sonic catharsis.

'School' was born of rage – of the anger that Cobain felt on discov-

ering that all the petty restrictions he had encountered while being fed through the education system were no different in the adult world, not least in the rock business. Only later would Cobain take a more measured line in his songwriting: 'School', all fifteen words of it, sounds like it was written in the mirror image of its subject matter, a petulant response to not getting his own way on some minor matter. It was instinctive, childish even, couched in self-pity: "Wouldn't you believe it, it's just my luck".

The chorus consisted of just two words, a murderous cry of "No recess". As Cobain explained in 1991, "'No recess' was just some surreal idea I had about being in school and being in social cliques all the time, and then you grow up having to deal with exactly the same things with your friends at parties and in clubs as you did in high school." Comments on other occasions made it clear that the song had been inspired by Seattle in general, and Sup Pop in particular. Out of Cobain's disrespect, a classic Seattle anthem was born.

Like 'About A Girl', 'School' enjoyed a longer life span than most of the *Bleach* material. A live version later appeared on the 'Come As You Are' CD/12" single.

LOVE BUZZ
(Robby Van Leeuwen)

KURT Cobain's sloppy attitude to rock's lyric content is nowhere better illustrated than here, a cover of an album track by late Sixties 'Venus' hitmakers Shocking Blue. The first verse and the chorus were all he wanted: more important was the song's fast-paced mock-Eastern riff, here given a decidedly rough ride.

Bassist Chris Novoselic first uncovered the song while the band was putting its set together late in 1987, and the cover soon became an integral and popular part of Nirvana's live repertoire – which makes its omission from the band's Reciprocal Studios demo session with Jack Endino in January 1988 somewhat surprising. When Jonathan Poneman suggested that the band record the song for their debut Sub Pop 45, the fact that they'd not already tried it out it in a studio helped explain the otherwise odd idea of starting their career with an obscure cover version.

'Love Buzz' was taped at a five-hour session on June 11, 1988, a productive day which also yielded the B-side, 'Big Cheese', plus 'Spank Thru' (issued later that year on the *Sub Pop 200* sampler) and 'Blandest' (considered for the flip before being dropped). It was drummer Chad Channing's first studio appearance with the band. The main bone of contention on the mix (finished on July 16) turned out to be Cobain's vocal, which Poneman asked to be re-recorded. Eager not to please, Kurt had also stuck a 45-second collage of voices culled from an old children's record at the start of the track, which Poneman's partner Pavitt gently suggested might be more effective if it was trimmed to just ten seconds. By the time 'Love Buzz' had made it onto LP, it had gone completely, and can now only be heard on the original hand-numbered, 1,000-only limited edition 45, the first in Sub Pop's 'Single Of The Month' club. This, Nirvana's recorded debut, was issued in October 1988, though its limited availability, while earning them some cult brownie points, clearly annoyed the band.

Described in Sub Pop's literature as "Heavy pop sludge from these untamed Olympia drop-ins", 'Love Buzz', with its flashy mock-Eastern riff and driving, upbeat manner, was one of the least musically oppressive moments in the band's early catalogue. However, by the time it appeared on single, in October 1988, all the smart talk in Seattle centred on Mudhoney, who had just followed up their near legendary 'Touch Me I'm Sick' 45 with the impressive *Superfuzz Bigmuff* album.

PAPER CUTS

LIKE 'FLOYD The Barber', 'Paper Cuts' was rescued and remixed from the original Reciprocal Studios demo that had been taped in January 1988 featuring the Melvins' Dale Crover on drums. That wasn't the only similarity: both songs shared in a graphic kind of horror story, quite different to Cobain's own horror story of alienation and personal distress. While Cobain based the gruesome events in 'Floyd The Barber' on a popular television show, the inspiration for 'Paper Cuts' had come straight out of his own real-life backwater home town of Aberdeen. While drifting aimlessly during much of 1985 and 1986, Cobain fell in with a local drug-dealer who, in time-honoured fashion, had a down-at-heel lackey by his side. This companion had come from a family of considerable local notoriety who'd been prosecuted for mistreating their children. Among the catalogue of abuses were locking them in one room with a pile of newspapers for a latrine, and feeding them by pushing food under the door.

Understandably, Cobain sang 'Paper Cuts' from the victim's perspective, and the musical backing ably reflects the ugliness of the subject matter. The stop-start unison playing of the guitar/bass/drums line-up is almost cruel in its repetitiveness, broken up only with howls of feedback and an odd bridge where Cobain sounds remarkably like Charles Hayward, of the little-known London-based avant-garde 'indy' band This Heat. (This Heat once released a song titled 'Paper Hats', which suggests that the comparison is worth mentioning.)

The song concludes with Cobain uttering an exasperated and rather sinister "Nirvana" several times, reinforcing the intended irony in his band's name.

NEGATIVE CREEP

A LATE hardcore anthem that would appeal to punks and stoners alike, 'Negative Creep' was a self-explanatory piece of simple self-analysis that the group mischievously segued with Creedence Clearwater Revival's 'Bad Moon Rising' in concert. In addition to the pithy and oft-repeated "I'm a negative creep and I'm stoned" line, Cobain threw in a competitive nod to Mudhoney's 'Sweet Young Thing' ('Sweet young thing ain't sweet no more') with 'Daddy's little girl ain't a girl no more". If consistent with the tenor of the song, this might well refer to an early sexual experience.

A fast-paced rent-a-riff crowd-pleaser, 'Negative Creep' was also notable for its faded ending – a rarity on early Nirvana songs.

SCOFF

N O DOUBT dynamic in concert, 'Scoff' again had an air of familiarity about it, right down to the common teenage complaint: "In my eyes I'm not lazy", and "In your eyes, I'm not worth it". Chided by his parents/elders, Cobain's attitude was to revel in his own worthlessness, prompting the repeated demand to "give me back my alcohol". The "Heal a million/Kill a million" chorus, though seemingly unrelated, connects this apparent waste of a single life to the anonymity hidden by human numbers.

SWAP MEET

WHILE metal riffs enjoy a higher profile on *Bleach* than the punk half of the Nirvana equation, 'Swap Meet' stands out with its jerky, post-punk rhythm, and Cobain's against-the-beat vocals. It doesn't start out that way: the song begins like another HM dirge, before settling on an undulating guitar figure that sounds remarkably like an inversion of the 'Love Buzz' riff.

A swap meet is like a car-boot sale but without the car. Small-time dealers set up tables loaded with their domestic cast-offs, or arts and craftsy home-mades, in a bid to make a few dollars. While not obviously lambasting or romanticising them, Cobain depicts two characters who aren't without emotion: they're simply unable to show it, whether love or bitterness. While this suggests a 'deadness' at the heart of rural American culture, there is a suspicion – he with his cigarettes, she with her photographs – that a side of Cobain secretly longed for the simplicities of such emotional detachment.

MR. MOUSTACHE

MOUSTACHES were never a great rock music accoutrement.

History suggests that these great hairy bogies seem only to sprout at moments when the music gets stale and backward looking. They epitomise mealy-mouthed conservatism. 'Mr. Moustache', driven by an insanely fast riff guaranteed to make a trucker put his foot down, takes an easy pot-shot at the all-American male, the one with "poop as hard as rock", the one who'll tell you, "yes I eat cow/I am not proud".

While writing material for *Bleach*, Cobain also doodled. One surviving scrap of paper features a four-window cartoon that shows a 'Mr. Moustache' at home with his gun, hunting trophies and can of beer. Awaiting the birth of his child, he says: "I want my very own honest, hard workin, Jew, spic, Nigger & faggot hatin 100% pure beef AMERICAN MALE! I'll teach him how to work on cars and exploit women." As the story continues, the child emerges to exact punishment on big daddy's face, summarising Cobain's own attitude to the world-dominating, world-wrecking Mr. Moustache.

SIFTING

ALTHOUGH the one-dimensional sound was beginning to grate by this stage in the album, at least the chorus of 'Sifting' elevated the song out of the aural mud, its tension/release effect being no less than a blueprint for the soft/loud style with which Nirvana later became synonymous. The song's length, almost five-and-a-half minutes, doesn't help, but relief comes in the form of a wailing, Blue Cheer-like acid-rock guitar break, which is unsatisfactorily buried in the mix.

Lyrically, this was a hasty late-night affair which gave little away, save for Cobain's love of wordplay and mistrust of authority figures such as teachers and preachers.

BIG CHEESE

PARENTS, teachers, men with moustaches. Sub Pop co-owner Jonathan Poneman was none of those, but once he'd talked Nirvana into recording a single for the label early in 1988, and started suggesting which songs ought to be on it, he became the latest in a long line of authority figures for Cobain to kick against. The singer later told biographer Michael Azerrad: "I was expressing all the pressures that I felt from him at the time because he was being so judgmental about what we were releasing."

Still, Nirvana got a great B-side out of it – after Poneman again demanded that Cobain re-record his vocals. Unusually, at this stage in the band's career, he double-tracked his voice during the chorus, and rather than the desperate, pleading cries that characterised his singing on *Bleach*, Cobain adopted a taunting, aggressive tone on 'Big Cheese'.

DOWNER

NOT INCLUDED on the original vinyl-only LP, 'Downer' first appeared as part of *Bleach* when the album was reissued on CD in 1992, in the wake of the group's success with *Nevermind*. It was one of the first Nirvana songs, originally recorded as an instrumental late in 1986 as part of the Fecal Matter home demo (taped with Melvins drummer Dale Crover). It got its first proper airing in April 1987, when the Olympia-based KAOS radio station broadcast half-a-dozen songs, when the incipient Nirvana was going out as Skid Row.

The version here was again culled from the January 1988 session recorded at Jack Endino's Reciprocal Studios with Dale Crover back in the drum-seat. Lyrically, it probably contained as many words as half the songs on the album put together – not that the meaning of the song was clearer than that of any other. In Azerrad's *Come As You Are* biography, Cobain came clean: "I was trying to be Mr Political Punk Rock Black Flag Guy. I really didn't know what I was talking about." He was right about the punk rock, too: the song's inclusion here is indicative of the group's spikier leanings in the early days. This was suppressed on much of *Bleach*, which opted for a thicker, hard rock sound – and got it. But it wasn't the last we heard about Nirvana's punk rock tendencies.

Nevermind

US and UK: Geffen DGCD 24425, September 1991

THREE SIGNIFICANT EVENTS TOOK PLACE BETWEEN THE RELEASE OF *BLEACH* AND the recording of *Nevermind*. Nirvana had been tempted away from Sub Pop, the small but aspirational independent record label that put Seattle on the map. They'd signed a lucrative deal with corporate heavyweights Geffen, which meant they could spend considerably more time (and money) working on a second LP with a name producer. And the merry-go-round of drummers that had seen several hopefuls occupy the hottest seat in the band had been resolved with the recruitment of Dave Grohl.

None of these changes could guarantee a hit record, let alone one that would redefine the sound of rock for the new decade. In fact, the most exciting thing about the continued ascent of *Nevermind* during the winter months of 1991/92 was that it seemed so unexpected. In the UK dance music seemed to have many of the best musical ideas; in the States, rap and hip-hop danced on the cutting-edge. After a mid-Eighties post-punk malaise, epitomised by the limp spectacle of Live Aid, rock had regained some of its disorder at the fringes, with grunge in the States and the short-lived shoegazing phenomenon in the UK. However, there was nothing at its commercial heart to suggest that it had regained its ability to enrapture in its time-honoured, high-spirited tradition.

Then Nirvana's *Nevermind* appeared, a blast of indie-forged dynamics made palatable to a wider audience via Kurt Cobain's fast blossoming talent for applying pure pop bodywork to a souped-up grunge engine. Assisted by the dynamic Dave Grohl, his gangly on-stage foil, Chris Novoselic, and the commercial nous of producer Butch Vig and engineer Andy Wallace, Cobain found himself at the helm of the finest rock machine to make headlines, enjoy critical favour and find commercial success since the Sex Pistols.

Over two years had passed between the release of *Bleach* and the arrival of *Nevermind* in the shops. Irrespective of the major changes already outlined above, Nirvana continued to build upon their small but jealously guarded fan base, which had picked up pockets of support via some steady touring (including several notable festival appearances), some friends in high rock critic places, and the occasional record. Cobain was every inch the Seattle slacker (unkempt and unwilling to play the game), Novoselic the student who seemed happy to slum it for a bit, and Dave Grohl the all-American kid who cheerfully went along with it all. In essence, Nirvana were a disparate trio that seemed destined for a year or two of cult celebrity before falling victim to the inevitable ebbs and flows of fashion.

Although often compared to both around the time of *Nevermind*, Nirvana were more Sex Pistols than Beatles, more charismatic front-man and his chaos-creating chums than a union of like-minded souls smiling their way to stardom. Less of an issue by this time was the band's roots in metal riffs of the most mind-crunching variety. Just months after *Bleach*, Cobain had warned of an imminent change of emphasis, telling a reporter that, "There won't be any songs as heavy as 'Paper Cuts' or 'Sifting' on the new record. That's just too boring. I'd rather have a good hook." On the face of it, that might have been a recipe for disappointment: plenty of bands get by with good hooks, but few have either the muscle or the individuality to make them count. There wasn't more than the merest suspicion that Nirvana would ever be one of those.

The first major step on the road to *Nevermind* was taken during one week in April 1990, when Nirvana travelled to Smart Studios, in Madison, Wisconsin, to work with one of the most rated producers of the new 'grunge' era. Butch Vig was a failed power-pop wannabe who'd seen his vintage gear-filled studio become a beacon for the new breed of noise makers. Killdozer, Laughing Hyenas, The Fluid, Smashing Pumpkins and Tad had all benefited from Vig's ability to make rock records sound like rock records ought to sound. He was a rarity in the modern producer's world in that he didn't go in for the ubiquitous 'big-haired' soundboard experience.

At the time of the initial Vig sessions, Nirvana were still thinking in terms of delivering their second Sub Pop album, provisionally entitled *Sheep*; and drummer Chad Channing was still in the band. Despite the fact that so much change was just around the corner, most of the performances recorded at these heavily bootlegged sessions bore a remarkable similarity to those that ended up on *Nevermind*. Even Dave Grohl later conceded that he basically repeated most of Channing's original drum parts.

The Smart sessions bore out Cobain's new hook-orientated statement with a vengeance. Nirvana's music was rarely hookless, often making a rant-a-long meal of Cobain's one-line choruses, but the new material was crafted on a quite different level of sophistication. Tracks recorded with Vig in April 1990 included 'Pay To Play' (which became 'Stay Away') (later issued in this original form on the DGC 'Rarities' CD in 1994), 'In Bloom' (which received an early airing later that year on the 'Sub Pop Video Network Program One' video, issued by Atavistic), 'Dive', 'Lithium', 'Sappy' (alias 'I Hate Myself And I Want To Die'), 'Polly' and 'Imodium' (which became 'Breed').

What had started life as a second album for an indie label was, by September 1990, regarded simply as a demo tape with which to court potential new backers. By then, Nirvana had shed Chad Channing at the end of a spring tour of America. After a short spell with Mudhoney's Dan Peters holding the sticks, the band recruited Dave Grohl ("the drummer of our dreams," said Cobain) from Washington DC hardcore band Scream.

Nirvana, who'd looked on as local heroes Mother Love Bone, Alice In Chains and Soundgarden all signed up to major labels, were also growing impatient with the cottage-industry-with-attitude that was Sub Pop. The catalyst for change was Sonic Youth, pathmakers for grunge whose wilfully experimental edge had prevented them from achieving the success they deserved. But they had signed to a major, and bassist Kim Gordon had recommended Nirvana to Mark Kates, Director of Alternative Music at Geffen's DGC subsidiary. He caught the band in action that autumn supporting Sonic Youth, and after fending off approaches from Capitol, Charisma and Columbia, announced in January 1991 that Nirvana was to sign to Geffen. The label had offered a $287,000 advance, which was smaller than Capitol's reputed $1 million, but built in a higher royalty. The deal was finally inked on April 30, 1991.

No one questioned the choice of material for the band's first major label album, which was to be based on the songs cut with Butch Vig at Smart in April 1990. There were, however, doubts concerning the appropriate choice of producer: Geffen preferred to see an experienced, commercially aware pair of hands on the controls, like Scott Litt or Don Dixon (both had smoothed R.E.M.'s passage into the mainstream), though the band were happy to stick with Vig. At one point, it looked like Dixon was going to get the job with Vig engineering, but eventually Geffen let the band have their way.

The label booked Nirvana and Butch Vig into the Sound City Studios, in the sleepy Los Angeles suburb of Van Nuys. The studio was, by then, somewhat unfashionable, but had seen better days in the Seventies, with Tom Petty, Foreigner and Rick Springfield all having recorded major albums there. The biggest ghost of all was that of Fleetwood Mac, who'd recorded their record-breaking *Rumours* album at Sound City, taking rock into new, sleepier AOR pastures in the process. That amused the band and Vig, who too was a major label debutante with this project. Cobain later described the studio as "a time machine".

The band met up with Vig in May 1991, and spent a week in rehearsal prior to the recording. The producer was also handed a tape that included material likely to feature during the sessions. Many he already knew from the Smart demo, but a couple of new songs, 'Smells Like Teen Spirit' and 'Come As You Are', caught his ear, despite the distorted sound quality of the primitively-recorded cassette.

The *Nevermind* sessions, which lasted six weeks in total, were completed in a convivial, almost carefree atmosphere, the kind that history seems to have excised from the Nirvana story. The band goofed around with Alice Cooper, Aerosmith and Black Sabbath covers, but when it was time to get their heads down, they worked hard and efficiently, often up to ten hours a day. The basic tracks were laid down in a matter of days, with much of the studio time being spent laying down overdubs – a problem the band rarely encountered during the making of *Bleach*. A nightly bottle of Jack Daniels, plus a jar of Hycomine cough syrup for the singer, helped to see them through.

Vig wasted no time in mixing the material, but Geffen weren't happy with the results, which were said to have lacked power, particularly in the drum department and drafted in Andy Wallace, an established mixing engineer who'd previously given Slayer's *Seasons In The Abyss* album an accessible sheen. He boosted the drum sound by adding digital reverb, and whacked the guitars and bass through a flanger. He then compressed the lot, so that the results would sound punchy and dynamic on radio. Hey presto, a more inviting album and by the way, your budget for the record has just doubled. It was one of the best investments Geffen ever made: the entire album had cost the label around half-a-million dollars from start to finish, but within two years, it had grossed in the region of £50 million – and that was before Kurt Cobain's death gave sales an inevitable new boost.

Cobain later remarked that he was embarrassed by the production, likening it to a Mötley Crüe record. But he was typically self-deprecating when it came to characterising the band's new sound for the record company press biog. "Our songs have the standard pop format," he told them, "verse, chorus, verse, chorus, solo, bad solo." And in an echo of his original handwritten bio for *Bleach*, he concluded: "All in all, we sound like The Knack and The Bay City Rollers being molested by Black Flag and Black Sabbath." The emphasis was now on pop being consumed by rock, rather than the other way round, which was had been the case with *Bleach*. Some critics took the results far more seriously, wondering whether we were witnessing the emergence of a new, industrial-strength version of The Beatles. But first there was Nirvanamania.

Geffen had envisaged *Nevermind* as the first strike in what was going to be a lengthy campaign to take the band from indie cult status to a popularity approaching R.E.M. proportions. That was the daydream. Within three weeks of the album's release, on September 24, 1991, *Nevermind* had far exceeded its projected sales of 50,000 by shipping 200,000 copies, more than Sonic Youth's major label debut *Goo* had sold in two years. In a similar period, *Bleach* had sold just 40,000.

Hitting the *Billboard* chart on October 12 at No. 144, the album's ascent was slow but certain. By the start of November, it nestled just outside the Top 30; by the end of the month, it had reached the Top ten; and on January 12, 1992, Nirvana had done the seemingly impossible, clambering over U2, Metallica and Michael Jackson to top the US chart. In the UK, Nirvanamania was slower to catch on, and less explosive in chart terms when it did, but *Nevermind* was still a regular fixture in the Top 30 for months.

Many reasons have been put forward in an attempt to explain just why Nirvana and *Nevermind* broke so big. MTV getting behind one of the songs, 'Smells Like Teen Spirit', was certainly a crucial factor in earning the band almost instant crossover appeal. And radio quickly got behind the album, so much so that journalist and biographer Gina Arnold quipped that Nirvana had indeed become an AOR band – Always On The Radio. But these factors refer merely to the power of the communications industry. While that's all-important – no exposure, no sales – it doesn't necessarily guarantee a hit.

Although both band and label claimed to have been taken by surprise by the soaraway success of the album, the bleached-out grunge, the punk-meets-metal, the artful blend of melodies and rage, were all deliberately concocted in the studio with a view to potential markets. *Nevermind* was a multi-purpose album that marked the coming of age of America's alternative rock scene, given a recent boost by the Lollapalooza tour. It regenerated a metal scene that was fast sliding into ineffective, poodle-haired posturing. And it breathed new dynamism into the melodic rock mainstream. Although Nirvana could predict which musical currents their music might reach, there was no doubt about the message behind the cover artwork, which was similarly stunning and memorable. Depicting the five-month-old Spencer Elden swimming towards a dollar bill on a fishhook, it played on the indie-versus-major debate, symbolising the group's willingness to take the corporate cash, whilst doubling as a general comment on a money-obsessed society. The retention of the baby's penis (Geffen were in two minds whether to airbrush it away) signalled some kind of victory. And the band's new T-shirt, bearing the "Flower-sniffin' kitty-pettin' baby-kissin' corporate rock whores" legend, poked self-conscious fun at their own new-found respectability. The laughter wouldn't last.

SMELLS LIKE TEEN SPIRIT
*(Kurt Cobain/Chris Novoselic/
Dave Grohl)*

THE ORIGINAL album sleeve credit-ed Cobain as the lyricist and the band for writing the music. By 1993, when the music was published in book form, Cobain had reneged on his benevolence, leaving just this song as a group composition. That was just as well for Novoselic and Grohl, because 'Smells Like Teen

Spirit' was and remains one of those rare songs that seems to define an era. It almost felt like that on first hearing, and the fact that everyone else seemed to share that view helped make it the fastest-spread-ing virus of late 1991.

Recalling the origins of 'Teen Spirit' and other *Nevermind* anthems, Cobain said, "At the time I was writing those songs, I really did-n't know what I was trying to say." Scrutinise the lyrics and you'll see exactly what he means, as seemingly unrelated phrases jostle to be sung, heard, yelled and scrawled onto banners at concerts, but rarely understood. What Cobain had succeeded in doing was to find a writing style that echoed the ultimately contradictory appeal of his music – intangible yet memorable, pleasurable yet inextricably bound up with some kind of inner pain.

These contrasts were built into 'Smells Like Teen Spirit': its central guitar motif, its measured, finely-tuned course from coasting verses into expansive choruses, could hardly have sounded more life-affirming. Lyrically, though, the mood couldn't have been more different: boredom, guns, pretence, a reluctant smile, and the climactic refrain of "a denial" encapsulated Cobain's dichotomy perfectly.

The song was inspired by a slogan scrawled on Cobain's bedroom wall in North Pear Street, Olympia, by another paramour, Bikini Kill's Kathleen Hanna, one night late in 1990. 'Kurt Smells Like Teen Spirit' was meant to be a sly dig, Teen Spirit being nothing so threatening as an underarm deodorant aimed at young women. But the phrase stuck, Cobain subconsciously (apparently) retrieved a riff from an old Boston hit from 1976, 'More Than A Feeling', and the track was formulated during the band's regular rehearsals in Tacoma that winter.

Later on, Cobain acknowledged another debt, telling *Rolling Stone* magazine in January 1994 that, "I was trying to write the ultimate pop song. I was basically trying to rip-off

the Pixies... We used their sense of dynamics, being soft and quiet and then loud and hard." While traces of that quiet/loud, soft/hard dynamic could be found on the band's earlier work, it was on *Nevermind* that Nirvana perfected the trick. But there was no doubt that listening to the Pixies' 1988 *Surfer Rosa* album (produced by Steve Albini) after recording *Bleach* left its impact.

When Nirvana debuted the song in Seattle in April 1991, there was little suggestion that 'Smells Like Teen Spirit' would soon be rotated on MTV an unprecedented ten times a day. Or that its possible meanings would be debated by ciderheads to champagne-supping yuppies. Or that 'Weird' Al Yankovic would parody it, and Tori Amos would record an opportunistic 'lounge' version of the song. By the time Nirvana returned to the UK to promote both single and the album, Cobain was bored enough with the song to sing it an octave lower for BBC-TV's *Top Of The Pops*, undercutting much of the song's power in the process. (He also changed the song's intro to "Load up on drugs and kill your friends".)

Months later, the band would tease audiences by playing the first few bars of the song before launching into something else. The irony of the line "Here we are now, entertain us" was impossible to maintain once superstardom called.

IN BLOOM

'IN BLOOM', the fourth single lifted from *Nevermind*, was one of the songs originally demoed with Butch Vig at Smart in April 1990. That version so impressed Sub Pop that it was issued on the *Sub Pop Video Network Program One* several months later, in order to promote the band (who, unknown to the label, were already intent on leaving).

It's not difficult to imagine 'In Bloom' performed *Bleach*-style, with the band going at the song hell-for-leather. Here, though, Vig and the band's original arrangement, and Wallace's delicate post-production work gave the song room to breathe; while Dave Grohl's harmony during the chorus accentuated the track's anthemic qualities.

Lyrically, 'In Bloom' poked fun at the small-town dude, the one who sings along to all the pretty songs, who happily shoots off his gun, but who dares not stop and think about his life: 'He knows not what it means'. While recording the album, around the time of the bombing of Baghdad, Chris Novoselic remembered having "such a feeling of us versus them. All those people waving the flag and being brainwashed. I really hated them. And all of a sudden they're buying our records, and I just think, 'You don't get it at all'." The in-concert mass chorusing along to 'In Bloom' (a favourite with Courtney Love, apparently) must have been a double-edged pleasure for the band.

COME AS YOU ARE

UNUSUALLY conciliatory in its subject matter, 'Come As You Are' was the song that Geffen envisaged would open up Nirvana to a new mass audience once 'Teen Spirit' had paved the way. As it turned out, the track sounded like a tame and strangely subdued follow-up, which seemed to grow in stature in the aftermath of Cobain's death: inevitably, a line like "And I swear that I don't have a gun" would hold new meaning, as would Cobain's plaintive "memory" hook.

The heavily flanged guitar sound, which gave the impression that the song had been recorded underwater, united the track with the album sleeve, a connection that was pursued in Kevin Kerslake's promo video. Cobain, who often made reference to his watery, swimming-in-opposite-directions Pisces star sign, was drugged at the time, but water – often symbolic of emotional turbulence – was becoming a recurrent theme in several of his songs.

Nirvana was the victim of a couple of law-suits during its short lifespan, but Killing Joke's claim that 'Come As You Are' had been based on a riff from their own 'Eighties' was rejected by the courts.

BREED

MUSIC analysts would characterise the album's first three songs as "moderate rock" (check the sheet music for proof). But there was no way that 'Breed', a piledriving, Bleach-on-speed offering, could ever fall into that category. Even the spartan lyric suggested this was a throwback to the band's debut album.

That wasn't far wrong, because the song was one of the earliest titles destined for Nevermind, written while the band were touring Europe with fellow Seattle labelmates Tad. It was Tad's hefty frontman, one Tad Doyle, who initially inspired the song, which was originally called 'Imodium' after the antidiarrhoea medicine the singer was forced to consume during the tour. It retained this title when the band first taped it with Vig in April 1990, and might well have made it onto disc that way had a second track not been named after a medicinal treatment.

LITHIUM

THAT SONG was 'Lithium', named after a treatment for depression, and later the cue for audiences to raise their lighters to show their communion with the track's central hook: "Yeah, yeah, yeah, yeah!" No surprise there: without Cobain's grainy rasp, and a musical twist midway through the song, 'Lithium' might easily have slotted onto any soft metal compilation.

That gibe doesn't do justice to the song's genuine beauty. The melody was neatly forged from a bare minimum of notes, while the lyric, one of the album's best, poetically negotiates the thin line between madness and the search for faith.

According to Cobain, 'Lithium' was "probably" inspired by the time he spent living with the family of his friend, Jesse Reed, during the summer of 1985. The Reed's lived a full, born-again Christian lifestyle, and the details of religious observance in the song are likely born of the experience.

Another song first taped with Butch Vig in 1990, 'Lithium' became the third single taken from Nevermind, and had the dubious honour of later being recorded by the original Nirvana, the psychedelicised late Sixties UK edition, who'd reformed in the early Nineties.

POLLY

MANY OF Cobain's earliest songs drew on real-life situations, often simply depressing, sometimes, like 'Paper Cuts', macabre and gruesome. 'Polly', which was written around the same time as much of Bleach, fell into the latter category, telling with some genuine insight, the horrific local story of the rape and torture of a 14-year-old pun-kette by the inappropriately named Gerald Friend.

Told from the rapist's stand-point, Cobain's lyric gets into the criminal's mind teasing out a series of 'justifications': "It isn't me/We have some seed", "the will of instinct", and finally, "I want some help to help myself". The full horror was brought home by the stark arrangement, featuring Cobain accompanying himself on acoustic guitar, which was the original Smart Studio, albeit in remixed form.

As if the song wasn't harrowing enough, 'Polly' itself was later sung by two men while raping a woman shortly after the release of *Nevermind*. Yet another depressing burden for the songwriter to bear, Cobain nevertheless didn't shy away from playing it – though few could ever hear it again without an additional layer of disbelief.

TERRITORIAL PISSINGS

DESPITE the muscular hard rock of the band's early records, Kurt Cobain was never short of some punk-inspired rhetoric. Here, at last, was the song to match it: fast, furi-ous and a match for almost any-thing released during the punk era. A regular cue for some on-stage mayhem, 'Territorial Pissings' gained further infamy in 1992 when the band tore into it during an appearance on a British television chat show hosted by Jonathan Ross.

This totally unscripted move left the presenter visibly shaken, and the same could probably be said of his audience, shocked by a rare injec-tion of televisual spontaneity. Nirvana's future in the UK was assured.

The song's distinct lack of gloss was down to Cobain's insistence that he plug his guitar directly into the mixing desk, despite Butch Vig's reluctance. This was a common punk rock production tac-tic, which gave the guitar an over-loaded sound. Coupled with a vocal that was audibly being cut to shreds with each successive verse, and some magnificent drumming from Grohl, 'Territorial Pissings', recorded in one take, remains a truly definitive Nirvana performance that deserved to have been issued on single.

The song's central lyric phrase, "Gotta find a way", seemed to fit the exuberant desperation of the per-formance, with its references to paranoia and Cobain's desires to be an alien. Those concerns also con-nect to the oddly comic intro, where Chris Novoselic tunelessly lam-poons a line from an old Youngbloods hippie anthem, 'Get Together', which gives way to Cobain's thrashy three-chord intro.

DRAIN YOU

'DRAIN YOU' welcomed back the happy, chart-bound production sound that characterised much of

Nevermind, and for whoever sequenced the record, it couldn't come soon enough, bounding in almost as soon as the final cymbal of 'Territorial Pissings' fades. If there is an air of familiarity about the song, it's because the verses are built on the same chord structure to 'Smells Like Teen Spirit', although the vocal is less equivocal in its celebratory tone. This isn't always reflected in the lyric, which charts the symbiotic relationship between two babies/lovers, who are seen to be governed not merely by love but by mutual dependency, even naked self-interest.

Cobain later said that he felt the song was every bit the equal of 'Teen Spirit' – and its appearance on the flip of that single, and in live form as a bonus cut on 'Come As You Are', seems to bear this out.

LOUNGE ACT

ONE OF the lesser-known songs on the album, 'Lounge Act' grew out of a jam based around a cheesy bass-line cooked up by Chris Novoselic. So cheesy, in fact, that the song that built up around it was so titled because the bassist's line was laughably reminiscent of an inoffensive hotel bar band.

By the time the song was completed, it sounded more like an Americanised version of British new wave, punk-inspired catch-a-wave acts like The Police: bouncy, energetic – and thoroughly inoffensive. It

was by no means Nirvana's finest moment, though Cobain's lyric gave some insight into the difficulties he faced maintaining relationships while giving total commitment to his creative vision.

STAY AWAY

IF KURT Cobain's lyrics tend to avoid the pitfalls of embarrassment that is often the lot of the hapless rock lyricist, that is largely down to his scatter-style approach, a stringing together of (often insightful) phrases that give the impression of being chemically induced. There is little anecdotal evidence to support this, save for the fact that Cobain's insecurity as a writer would have been overcome by mind-unlocking influences.

The curt couplets of 'Stay Away' seem to suggest this more than most songs. 'Every line ends in rhyme/Less is more, love is blind', and 'Throw it out and keep it in/Have to have poison skin' *could* have come from the pen of any doodling dreamer. But the vision of Cobain in his pyjamas, cup of tea by his side, agonising over lines like those – though by all accounts he *did* agonise over his lyrics, which further suggests the need for 'unblocking' agents – doesn't ring true.

'Stay Away', which first surfaced as a riff on the 1986 *Fecal Matter* demo, had one of the longest gestation periods of all Nirvana songs. By 1990, it was ready – as 'Pay To Play' – for Butch Vig to record at the Smart Studios sessions, at which stage the song featured slightly different lyrics, more feedback and a coda. By the time it was recorded for *Nevermind* as 'Stay Away', it had been transformed from a put-down of an unscrupulous practice initiated by concert promoters during the Eighties, to a partial critique of rock band infighting.

Less sophisticated melodically than much of the *Nevermind* material, and lacking the relentless onslaught of 'Territorial Pissings', 'Stay Away' was another of the album's more anonymous tracks – though it would have been difficult to say that had it appeared on any other album at the time.

The original Butch Vig recording of 'Pay To Play' eventually turned up on the 'DGC Rarities Volume One' various artists compilation in 1994.

ON A PLAIN

THE FEW seconds of tune-up noise that introduced this song were deceiving: 'On A Plain' was one of the album's real moments of glorious power-pop release – upbeat, instantly memorable and even rejoicing in a call-and-response chorus (of sorts). Even Cobain was moved to sing an uncharacteristic "I can't complain".

The only trace of angst in the song came with the admission that

"I love myself better than you/I know it's wrong, but what should I do?" In fact, the lyrics comprised a few hastily dashed-off lines, written immediately prior to the recording session, which made it clear that Cobain had grown exhausted having to find words to fit his tunes. How else does one read a song that opens with the words, "I'll start this off without any words", and closes with "Then I'm done, then I can go home"?

SOMETHING IN THE WAY

THIS WAS one of the last tracks to be written for *Nevermind* and, placed at the end of the album, it encouraged the listener to leave with a quite different impression of the supercharged rock band they'd been listening to for the past forty minutes. Rock tradition often dictates that album's parting gestures are either rip-roaringly typical of the artist's style, or if different, then indicative of a bold new direction being staked out. Certainly, there was more from where 'Something In The Way' came from on Nirvana's next studio album.

The song was an exercise in self-mythology, with Cobain revisiting his brief period of homelessness in Aberdeen late in 1985. Forced to leave the flat he shared with Jesse Reed, and mindful of overstaying his welcome at the Novoselics' family home, Cobain spent a few nights sleeping under the North Aberdeen

Bridge (which crossed the Wishkah river) surviving on wood fire for heat and cheap red wine for fortification. There is something about the romance of the drifter's life, free from responsibility and with civilisation in the distance, which suggests that Cobain's decision to rough it wasn't entirely an involuntary one.

Whatever the truth, he got a great song out of the experience, again a latecomer to the *Nevermind* sessions. Never intended to be so sparse, 'Something In The Way' nearly didn't make it onto the record, after endless attempts to find a satisfactory band arrangement proved inconclusive. It was only when Butch Vig asked Cobain to play the song for him on an acoustic guitar in his control-room that the arrangement became clear: Vig taped Cobain's performance there and then. The band's overdubs, and a mournful cello part played by Kirk Canning, were added later.

ENDLESS, NAMELESS

IN 'SOMETHING In The Way', Nirvana had chosen to end the album in an uncharacteristic manner that may or may not have suggested that some drastic musical changes were afoot. But through a clever piece of digital trickery, they were also able to have it both ways, hiding a 'secret' bonus track some ten minutes after 'Something In The Way' had finished. (Soon afterwards, it seemed

as if every second new CD release came with a 'hidden' track.)

Sometimes called 'The Noise Jam', 'Endless, Nameless' came about at the end of a none-too-successful session for 'Lithium'. The sound of three musicians practising primal therapy through their instruments, this largely wordless jam (Cobain shrieks something like 'I think I can/I know I can' for a short while) wasn't entirely spontaneous; the group had been playing something like it for several months. And just as similar on-stage free-for-alls ended with the sound of equipment being trashed, so, at somewhere around 19.32 on the track, Cobain's guitar can be heard disintegrating.

Just to confuse their new-found pop fans, Nirvana selected 'Endless, Nameless' to back the 'Come As You Are' single – a move that was also welcomed by early purchasers of *Nevermind*, who were cheated out of the song. And perhaps its belated appearance meant that Nirvana were having second thoughts, that their next album would be more hardcore?

In Utero

Geffen GED 24536, September 1993

THERE WERE TWO CONFLICTING EXPECTATIONS OF *IN UTERO*. THE BULK OF Nirvana's post-'Teen Spirit' audience, for whom Cobain had little regard, expected what mass audiences always want – more of the same. When word spread that *In Utero* was as unpolished and as ungainly as *Nevermind* had been airbrushed for mass consumption, its sales curve did the exact opposite to that of its predecessor. Rarely had a rock band bit the hand that fed them so spectacularly. (Other notable examples have included the Fab Foursome's mystifying *Magical Mystery Tour* film, televised during Christmas 1967 to an audience baffled by its lack of plot and psychedelic in-jokes; and ex-Sex Pistol John Lydon's debut album with PiL, which singed the bumfluff from many a young punk's upper lip.)

Others applauded Nirvana's decision to work with engineer Steve Albini as a welcome reversal of the traditional rock'n'roll trajectory – get noticed by building a cult audience on an indie label, take the corporate bait with promises of "No sell out!", develop a taste for a celebrity lifestyle, and make increasingly anodyne records in order to sell enough copies to maintain it. Cobain was acutely aware of the demeaning, if likely, future that awaited him, but while uneasy with his new status, he wasn't about to alight the gravy train and rejoin the ranks of the Great Impoverished.

This, more than any other record of his, presented Cobain with a dilemma. He was was caught between his own conscience, and his desire to avoid the indignity of releasing a record which would be panned by the majority of critics and prove unpalatable to fans of *Nevermind*. As soon as sessions for the album were over, he was claiming that the results would be "exactly the kind of record I would buy as a fan". Within a month, he had changed his tune, claiming that the album was "not as good" as *Nevermind*.

The consequence was two highly publicised spats between, first the band and Geffen, and then Cobain and Albini. All of this made *In Utero*, already one of the most eagerly awaited albums in years, also one of the most controversial. The record hit number one immediately on its release, but couldn't hope to rival *Nevermind*, either in terms of cultural effect or commercial clout. Yet it remains Nirvana's most accomplished album, being neither the impenetrable noise-fest feared by the band's management structure, nor the sanitised hardcore expected by those who suspected that too much rested on the album's commercial success.

Even when the repercussions of *Nevermind* were still being felt the world over, Kurt Cobain was distancing himself from the album, regarding it as "a complete sell-out" and "a complete betrayal of the punk ethos". By

June 1992, Geffen had circulated a press release that set pulses racing among the band's more outré fan contingent. Giving a new spin on the bullishness that usually accompanies rags-to-riches success, it claimed that the next Nirvana record would not even pretend to emulate its predecessor. Instead, the album, provisionally and controversially titled *I Hate Myself And I Want To Die*, would disregard all the expectations aroused by *Nevermind*. The implication was that the months of compromise were over. It was time to meet the real Nirvana.

By early 1994, once the album had been and gone, Cobain was quizzed about the original title. "As literal as a joke can be. Nothing more than a joke," he responded. "I thought it was a funny title. I wanted it to be the title of the album for a long time. But I knew the majority of the people wouldn't understand it." This attempt to make light of a title that some suggested was a band in-joke wasn't accepted by many, even before the events of April 1994. William Burroughs, who collaborated with Cobain on a 1993 single, needed only one look at the album's lyrics before pronouncing the singer to be "dead already" by the time he wrote them.

Cobain had several *In Utero* songs in the bag as early as March 1992, with three, 'Rape Me', 'Dumb' and 'Pennyroyal Tea', having been in circulation among fans and insiders within weeks of the release of *Nevermind*. That was just as well, for 1992 proved to be the most traumatic year in Cobain's life.

It began with Nirvana being the most talked about group in years, and ended with Cobain and his wife Courtney Love being the most controversial celebrity twosome since, oh, Sid'n'Nancy. During the interim, the couple married amidst rumours of unrest within the Nirvana camp (Chris Novoselic didn't attend the wedding). Cobain collapsed with what was described as a "mystery virus" during a short European tour. The band were sued by Killing Joke, who claimed plagiarism, and by the original Nirvana, a Sixties UK psychedelic duo. *Vanity Fair* magazine penned an unflattering portrait of the soon-to-be Cobain parents. The birth of Frances Bean Cobain yielded scaremongering reports in American scandal-sheets that the baby was "a junkie". Cobain touted a loosely anti-drug stance in public, while privately, rumours of a more than passing flirtation with 'Mr. Brownstone' circulated. Julian Cope paid good money to diss Courtney in press adverts, claiming she was a "Nancy Spungen fixated heroin a-hole". And the Cobains dealt with the 'problem' of unofficial biographers Britt Collins and Victoria Clarke by leaving a series of threatening messages on the pair's answering-machine.

Taken individually, these controversies might be regarded as par for the course, where a bit of rock star petulance meets some traditional media dirt-digging. Collectively, they pointed towards a near-pathological fixation with a life (or lives) running out of control under the pressure of the public

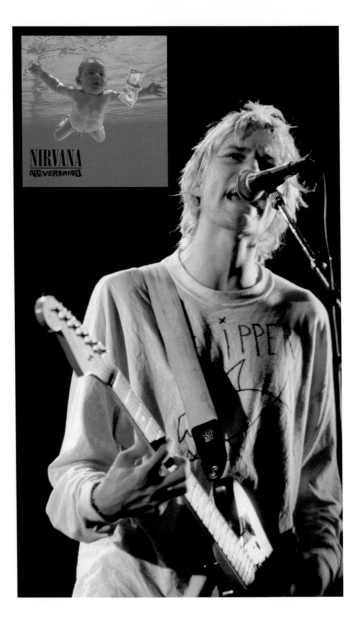

gaze. Rather than being excised, and comforted by his new found fame, the inner demons that Cobain had been struggling with since his youth had instead become magnified. He no longer had himself to contend with, but a self that kept spinning back to him in increasingly unrecognisable media forms. He also had a family to protect, expectations to live up to, and a large industry support-structure dependent on his every move. The only vent he had for his private melancholia was his next record, every word and note of which would be scanned for hints as to his current state of mind. Cobain fully understood that, and responded by introducing elements of gameplay into *In Utero*, which was otherwise an open letter from a morbid heart.

Steve Albini himself was no stranger to controversy. The Chicago-based guitarist/engineer had a reputation as one of the most single-minded, opinionated and gifted figures in American hardcore during the Eighties by virtue of his band Big Black, a trio who invested the dynamics of original punk rock with the punishment levels of Industrial music pioneers Throbbing Gristle. On the cusp of mainstream indie crossover success, Albini split the band to form Rapeman, who took the Big Black ethos a stage further by incorporating real drums instead of a drum-machine. However, the name quickly overshadowed the group's musical virtues, and the group folded, with Albini moving into production (or 'engineering', as he preferred to call it). His work had not gone unnoticed by Cobain. Albini had overseen sessions for the Pixies' *Surfer Rosa*, a record whose soft/loud dynamics had proved such an influence on *Nevermind* in general, and 'Smells Like Teen Spirit' in particular. More than that, he presented a persona that was in direct opposition to Kurt's 'Piscean failure' demeanour. It's tempting to speculate that Albini performed a similar role in the studio to the one Courtney Love assumed in his daily life, investing Cobain with power by proxy. Albini's self-bestowed 'engineer' status suggests a hands-off approach to recording, simply allowing the band the opportunity to emerge with a record that sounded as raw and as magnificent as a sparkling first take. Anecdotes about the engineer keeping the band amused by igniting his farts in the studio (smells like teen antics) probably make light of the conspiratorial sense of authority his involvement brought to the sessions.

Albini, like Cobain, also carried a mystifying (at least to UK audiences weaned on punk rock) torch to the ass-kicking production of mid-Seventies US rock – to the point of gleefully admitting that the 24-track analogue, Neve mixing-desk in his Pachyderm Studios was once used to record AC/DC's *Back In Black*. Cobain drew parallels between Albini's work on the Pixies' *Surfer Rosa* and the Breeders' *Pod* albums with the drum sound on Aerosmith's 1976 *Rocks* LP, a sense of rock geography that is largely lost on UK audiences. But there were inevitable tensions, not least in Albini's early dismissal of Nirvana as "R.E.M. with a fuzzbox", which from his perspective was definitely not a compliment.

Nirvana booked into Pachyderm, the Minnesota studio that lay some fifty miles south of Minneapolis, as the Simon Ritchie Group, a reference to the Sid'n'Nancy-type depiction of Cobain and Love in the press. Despite the traumas of the previous twelve months, the sessions, which began at the start of the third week in February 1993, were remarkably trouble-free. The basics for the dozen or so tracks, plus a couple of out-takes were laid down in just six days, with most of the vocals added in one day-long session. Within two weeks, the third and final Nirvana studio album was completed; and both band and producer were happy with the results. The studio bill was a paltry $24,000, with Albini collecting a one-off $100,000 fee.

Albini later suggested that had he been the kind of producer who demanded total control, he would have mixed the vocals lower in the mix, but let this pass in deference to his ideological commitment to letting the band have the final say. At least the layers of vocals that characterised the 'overproduced' sound of *Nevermind* were absent.

By the time work had been completed, the album's title had been changed to *Verse Chorus Verse*. Eschewing existential disturbance for a sardonic gibe at a winning musical formula, it was mildly misleading and self-referentially iconoclastic. A fair percentage of the material recorded with Albini conformed to the standard rock and pop rules of song construction that unite everyone from Guns N' Roses to Kylie Minogue.

By late May, the title had changed once more, this time to *In Utero*, a gynaecological reference apparently culled from a poem written by Courtney Love. More than that, Cobain and Novoselic (by now affirming his Croatian roots by reverting to his birthname Krist) in particular were having second thoughts about the overall sound of the record. The bass frequencies were too murky, and the vocals were still too low in the mix. The folks at Geffen were apparently horrified. Albini, in an attempt to call the band's bluff, informed the *Chicago Herald* that, "I have no faith this album will ever be released".

Scott Litt, best known for his work with R.E.M., was invited to perform a quick makeover job in May, remixing the album's two potential singles, 'Heart-Shaped Box' and 'All Apologies', to these new specifications. The Seventies AOR rock connection was, however, maintained, as this took place in the Bad Animals Studios, which was owned by the Wilson sisters of Heart fame. Litt also oversaw the entire remastering process, giving the vocals a general boost, adding more top-end to the bass, and compressing the lot in a bid to appease radio producers. By the time the cover art was being prepared, Nirvana had added their preferential treble and bass settings, boosting both into overdrive.

Already the subject of an interminably fraught birth, *In Utero* found no greater ease in the early days of its shelf life. Within days of its release, two major American national retailers, including Wal-Mart, refused to stock it. The problem seemed to be Cobain's back cover collage of plastic foetuses, lilies and orchids. (Never mind that almost every lyric contained a ...ness and diseased state of mind culled from Cobain's recent ...ences of the world in which he found himself.) And so for the good ...of Middle America, whose lives were made complete by a ...c admonishing of the struggles of others, 'Rape Me' became 'Waif ...e offending foetuses were carefully removed. Fictions such as ...Baby Born A Junkie" headlines were OK, it seemed; images ... the origin of life were not. And this from the kind of people ...that Cobain was fucked up...

SERVE THE SERVANTS

ALL THE traumas that surrounded the making of the album were immediately kicked into touch by the first bars of 'Serve The Servants'. No sooner had the playful opening discord faded, than the song stabilised around an upbeat riff that made light of all the doomsday scenario talk. The track was as close to conventional rock'n'roll as Nirvana ever got, with only the suspicion that it could have been taken at a marginally faster pace locating it within a characteristically 'slacker' setting. What's more, its structure exactly mirrored the 'verse, chorus, verse' pattern that Cobain had threatened to lampoon, and possibly even jettison. What subversion there was came by way of the mild inversion of the soft/loud trick that had elevated the choruses of the anthems on *Nevermind*. On this occasion, it was the verses that cooked up the storm, while the cho-

rus refrains sounded effortless and subdued.

Lyrically, 'Serve The Servants' set the tone for the album, which was more wordy and rich in autobiographical references than before. The opening "Teenage angst has paid off well/Now I'm bored and old" line encapsulated Cobain's entire predicament. Not only did it acknowledge the cynicism that inevitably lies in wait for those who've crossed the great divide from indie ghetto to mainstream acceptance; it also seemed to embrace it. In doing so, Cobain was able to fortify himself with the armour of clear-eyed self-reflection, while revealing himself as his own harshest critic. The effect was humorous more than anything else, but the direct links between the sentiment and Cobain's quoting of Neil Young's "It's better to burn out than to fade away" lyric at the end of his suicide-note revealed the truths contained in his apparent jest.

Elsewhere, the song rails in other important directions. The parallels between the persecution of witches in the Middle Ages and the press treatment of Courtney Love were obvious. The reference to his parents' "legendary divorce" being "such a bore" showed impatience at his own mythology. But this was undermined in the second verse, which again damns his father, while making some attempt to recast that fraught relationship in a marginally more favourable light ("I just want you to know that I don't hate you any more").

SCENTLESS APPRENTICE

WHEN critics sought to describe the music of the Steve Albini-fronted Big Black, the words "punishing" and "relentless" immediately sprang to mind. 'Scentless Apprentice', cooked up during rehearsals for the album, was unquestionably Nirvana's take on Albini's method, right down to the sneering vocal delivery. It was the first evidence that the band were prepared to take an uncompromising stance, to nail their mast to the sounds of the American hardcore underground where intricate songwriting techniques were eschewed in favour of embracing the sheer pleasures of power-trio noise.

Whereas so much of *Nevermind* invited audiences in with its hooks and production niceties, 'Scentless Apprentice' was the sonic equivalent of the one-finger salute, its raw, abrasive sound and skull-crushing

riff the perfect mirror to Cobain's alienated lyric. Odd, then, that the song was one of the few genuinely collaborative efforts in the Nirvana catalogue: Dave Grohl came up with the riff (which Cobain initially denounced as too Tad-like), while Krist Novoselic came up with the song's second section.

Cobain's main contribution was the flurry of ascending guitar notes, and the lyric, which was based – uncharacteristically – on a book by German novelist Patrick Süsskind. Titled *Perfume*, and published in 1986, it combined two of Cobain's overriding preoccupations – bodily functions and misanthropy. The 'Scentless Apprentice' is based on the book's central character, who is born with an acute sense of smell but gives off absolutely no odour himself. This peculiar talent soon finds him apprenticed to a perfume maker. Meanwhile, he develops an extreme disgust for the smell of humans (echoing playwright Antonin Artaud's "Where there is the stink of shit, there is the smell of being" dictum).

Discussing the book's direct inspiration for the song, Cobain told biographer Michael Azerrad that, "I just wanted to be as far away from people as I could. Their smell disgusts me. The scent of human." Sixty years earlier, another infamous iconoclast, Greta Garbo, articulated her alienation with a polite, "I want to be alone". Cobain took advantage of the full range of late twentieth century expression with a murderous "Go awaaaay!" – several times

...ring the song. It's probably a sad ... the contemporary

remixed by Scott Litt three months after the Albini sessions had fin-... Cobain also took the opportu-

shelves. Chief among these were dozens of heart-shaped boxes, totems of the couple's mutual love ever since Courtney gave one to Kurt during their early courting days (that particular specimen was pictured on the sleeve for the 'Heart-Shaped Box' single). That the image doubled as a vagina probably wasn't lost on them, either, a reference reinforced by the invocation of "meat-eating orchids", another vagina metaphor in Cobain's language, and the reference to "broken hymen of your highness".

The song returned to the standard Nirvana trick of juxtaposing softly-sung verses with a rousing, HM-friendly chorus, without ever threatening to emulate the sheer exhilaration of a 'Teen Spirit' or a 'Lithium'. The tension was taut, but veered too close to hard-rock cliché to ever become one of the more memorable moments in the Nirvana canon. It did, however, sound more like a single than most of the other *In Utero* tracks, which is why it was one of two songs

sessions, everything fell into p... the mellow vocal line during the verses, Krist Novoselic's spiralling bass-line during the chorus – although the original take with Albini also featured an effects-draped guitar solo throughout the song which was later removed from the final mix.

While ostensibly about his relationship with Love – he the weak Piscean, she the pillar of strength with the "priceless advice" – Cobain also told interviewers that the song was partially inspired after seeing a documentary on children living with terminal cancer. His own oft-discussed illnesses were also cited ("Hey! Wait! I've got a new complaint"), not least the fact that he'd been born against his own will ("Throw down your umbilical noose so I can climb right back").

RAPE ME

'SMELLS LIKE Teen Spirit' had almost single-handedly transformed Nirvana from local heroes to international workhorses. What greater act of subversion, then, than to take every budding guitarist's favourite chord pattern, mash it up a little, and top it with a lyric that scorned the celebrity it brought with a vicious metaphorical twist. On the face of it, that's exactly what 'Rape Me' was about: from a position of almost unfathomable cultural power, Cobain threw his role as Commodity Fetish Number One, there to be abused until the next willing victim came along, back into the face of his public.

Like all his deliberations from within the heart of the commercial beast, it only rang partially true. If his stardom was as unwanted, and as complicated as he had often maintained, then why not retire quietly to some celebrity hideaway on the proceeds of one of the most successful albums in recent times? Because that ignores the fact that Cobain was an idealist at heart: on the one hand, he'd yearn for the simple world-view of a child, but the opportunity to lay bare the mean-minded adult world always proved irresistible. Perhaps it might even sit up and take notice?

Although 'Rape Me' fitted Cobain's jaundiced view of his own success perfectly, the song was written long before the world's media demanded a piece of him, during the mixing of *Nevermind* in mid-1991. At the time, it was simply an extension of 'Polly', "a song that supported women and dealt with the issue of rape", he later told *Rolling Stone*. Its message was easily misconstrued, as evidenced by the fact that women's groups were among those who initially objected to the song when the album appeared. The numbskull attitude shown by a couple of Nirvana 'fans' who'd sung 'Polly' while raping a woman didn't prevent Cobain from titling a new song 'Rape Me'. Some cried "Irresponsible!", but Cobain likely took perverse delight in thinking it wasn't the song, but society's prevailing values and attitude to women that is truly fucked up.

He used the song to settle another score, the sardonic reference to his "favourite source" who'll "always stink and burn", a clear dig at a manager of another top Seattle band who he felt had been feeding the press with dirt on him and his wife. When it became clear that 'Rape Me' prevented a couple of major record chains in the States from stocking the album, Geffen quickly altered the title to 'Waif Me'. (That was after the group playfully considered offering 'Sexually Assault Me' as an alternate title.)

FRANCES FARMER WILL HAVE HER REVENGE ON SEATTLE

Depending on which account you believe, Kurt Cobain either read William Arnold's biography, *Shadowland*, at school in 1978, or during the winter of 1990. Perhaps he read it twice. After all, the traumatic life of the Communist-sympathising, Hollywood-baiting, Seattle-raised actress who took refuge in drink and drugs in a bid to escape persecution increasingly mirrored his own.

Once again, he invoked the medieval "float or drown" witch's test, seeing in Farmer's case all the hallmarks of a modern-day witch-hunt. Both he and Love denied the suggestion that their baby daughter had been named after the tragic heroine. It was largely in vain — Courtney married Cobain wearing a lace dress originally owned by Farmer, and Kurt's unsuccessful attempts to contact the author of her biography during the last weeks of his life made his fascination for Farmer all the more obvious. Forever guilt-laden, it has been suggested by at least one author that Kurt believed he was distantly related to the judge who had her committed to an asylum during the Forties.

The song's chief refrain, "I miss the comfort in being sad", probably referred to the sense of empathy and indignation he felt while reading Arnold's exposé. As another one of his heroes Johnny Rotten once sang, anger is, after all, an energy.

DUMB

If Rock'n'Roll provides the best opportunity for aggrieved souls to find some satisfaction in a life that otherwise offers either financial or spiritual poverty, the other obvious outlet is through drink and drugs. Dumb, perhaps, but an essential protection from the mundane horrors of normality. Cobain, who was undoubtedly tuned in to emotional peaks and troughs more acutely than most, sought solace in them all, his festering rage best tempered by the simple pleasures of sky-high stimulants.

'Dumb' celebrates this near-religious desire for chemically-induced escape with a frivolity that's often been undervalued in his work, his "The sun is gone/But I have a light" couplet being one of the more memorable references to the joys of ciggie-smoking in rock (tobacco being akin to oxygen to Cobain).

While he constantly required the crutch of narcotics to blot out pain and remind him of joy, Cobain probably envied those who could get by simply with less physically-damaging pursuits. When discussing the song in 1993, he remarked that it was "just about people who're easily amused, people who not only aren't capable of progressing their intelligence but are totally happy watching ten hours of television and really enjoy it." His wish, he said was to be able to take a pill that would allow him to be amused by television "and enjoy the simple things in life, instead of being so judgmental and expecting real good quality instead of shit". The less charitable might claim that he was merely being pompous, that this professed "ignorance is bliss" philosophy was counter to all his own acts of self-transformation. Maybe so, but Cobain was in no position to un-learn all that he'd discovered: his cynicism stuck to him like the glue he celebrated in the song.

'Dumb' remains one of the most delicate songs in the entire Nirvana canon, evocative of The Beatles in their more baroque, melancholy moments (viz. 'Eleanor Rigby'), a connection underscored by the deployment of cellist Kera Schaley. The track was another renegade from the summer of 1990, and was debuted on the Washington alternative station Radio KAOS.

VERY APE

Ray Davies' 'Apeman' and Bowie's "Look at those cavemen go" ('Life On Mars') are two of the more memorable rock'n'roll references to the brutality of unreconstituted man, both of which probably do apes and prehistoric man a disservice. Cobain had earlier vented his spleen on proletarian bruiser culture on *Bleach*

('Mr. Moustache'), and this throwaway track, concocted during the *In Utero* sessions, was no more sophisticated than either that song or the subject matter.

Melvins' bassist Matt Lukin once said that Kurt "was terrified of jocks and moron dudes", although the boundary between admonishing persons unknown and self-critique is more blurred here. Take the first words of the song: "I am buried up to my neck in contradictory flies", which was as neat an encapsulation of the Cobain psyche as one could find on a Nirvana record. This sentiment was mirrored in the song's brief gestation: starting life as 'Perky New Wave Number', it soon ended up sounding more like a metal band cast-off.

MILK IT

The DUAL nature of Nirvana's music, a symbiotic union of the soft and the hard, was explored more thoroughly on 'Milk It', with little evidence of the radio-friendly hooks that had delivered songs like 'Come As You Are' and 'Smells Like Teen Spirit' to mainstream audiences.

The track starts out as if it has just stepped into the middle of a Grateful Dead jam, Cobain's spidery guitar lines playing freely over a stop-start rhythm. Although the song's central focus was an undulating, hammerhead power-trio riff, the regular collapse into quiet passages of instrumental exploration indicated that the band was keen to carve out new space to move in. Those tentative passages gave the main riff all the more impact when it arrived, topped with a vocal that shrieked with flailing desperation.

Once again, the lyric betrays an abiding obsession with disease (and bodily fluids/substances), increasingly the only aspect of himself Cobain had some kind of control over. "Look on the bright side (is) suicide" he raged as the song hit its peaking moments.

PENNYROYAL TEA

IF 'SMELLS Like Teen Spirit' was the defining track on *Nevermind*, then that honour probably went to 'Pennyroyal Tea' on *In Utero*. Any perceived shift from spirits to tea was a red herring, though, for despite the song's title – with its connotations of a blue-rinse tea-room in an English country garden – at the song's heart was the same sense of dysfunction that pervaded the entire record. Even the song's subject wasn't as anodyne as it sounded: Pennyroyal tea was a herbal treatment for abortion, and one with an unreliable track-record.

The song was written while Cobain shared a flat with new boy Dave Grohl in North Peak Street, Olympia. The pair recorded what was apparently a genuinely collaborative effort (Grohl is said to have come up with the melody) on four-

track, but Cobain felt that it wasn't developed enough to consider for *Nevermind*. That decision turned out to be prescient, for the song's subject matter fitted the mood of *In Utero* perfectly, by which time Cobain's psychic and mental scars were common knowledge.

One difference is that the chord structures were more conventional, more Beatles than Buzzcocks, although that was deceptive in terms of the song's visceral power. Despite the outstanding results, with Nirvana's trademark soft/hard conflict resolved as each verse effortlessly glided into the chorus, Cobain thought the finished product didn't do the song justice. "That should have been recorded like *Nevermind*, because it's a strong song, a hit single," he later remarked, going as far as posting a message on the Internet on March 27, 1994 saying that he planned to revamp the song. Whether he would have done so or not, the fact that Geffen pressed up a batch of promotional CDs suggested that the song was likely to have been the follow-up single to 'All Apologies'.

While Cobain often dressed his self-loathing up in industrial-strength riffs and anguished vocal lines, 'Pennyroyal Tea' was plaintive, almost rueful, expunging loneliness with almost childish self-pity. That's him in the corner, hunched awkwardly listening to Leonard Cohen and idly musing on the afterlife, with only his Pennyroyal tea (or "heroin and laxatives", as he sometimes sang in concert) for comfort;

hating himself and wanting to die, but strangely not wishing it any other way.

RADIO FRIENDLY UNIT SHIFTER

SOMETIMES dismissed as one of the album's "filler" tracks, 'Radio Friendly Unit Shifter' harked back to the relentless drive of the *Bleach* material. It benefits immeasurably from Albini's seriously hardcore production, some waywardly flanged guitar overdubs, and a lyric that expresses Cobain's uncomfortable relationship with the material spoils of his "unit-shifting" success.

Although Cobain was constantly hailed as the man who united melody with the abrasive qualities of punk and metal, sometimes there's nothing more potent than joining a single riff with one memorable lyric motif ("What is wrong with me?"). Separate Grohl's drumming, which sounds like a Motown session man with a rocket up his backside, and Novoselic's bass, which could have been lifted from an early Seventies Miles Davis excursion into funk, and the track sounds less like filler and more like a multi-dimensional *tour de force*.

TOURETTE'S

ONE OF the last songs to be readied for the album, 'Tourette's'

was pure punk rock – indecipherable (and unprinted) lyrics, save for a cursory "Cufk", "Tish" and "Sips" on the lyric sheet, a 'Territorial Pissings'-like three-chord thrash, and all over in just over one-and-a-half minutes. Its title was taken from a disorder that provokes involuntary displays of anti-social behaviour. That these utterances and gestures are often more profane than sacred suggests that those with the syndrome have an intuitive knack of expressing the apparently inexpressible – an "affliction" that had obvious appeal to an exposé merchant like Cobain.

The track even starts out like 'Territorial Pissings', with Krist Novoselic intoning "moderate rock" (a phrase used by more Nirvana sheet music analysts than the band would have liked), before a burst of signal noise gives way to a distortion-racked riff. This breaks up intermittently to revisit a guitar refrain straight out of Seventies' art-glam hipsters Sparks' 'This Town Ain't Big Enough For The Both Of Us'. For what it's worth, the track began life as 'Chuck Chuck'.

ALL APOLOGIES

IF 'PENNYROYAL Tea' was the album's heart, 'All Apologies' was its soul, occupying a similar role to 'About A Girl' on *Bleach* and 'Something In The Way' on *Nevermind*. Amid a record already close to OD'ing on guilt and self-loathing, 'All Apologies' is part suicide-note, part a quest for the kind of universal karma that inspired original Grateful Dead fans to hitch a ride to the Far East in search of spiritual contentment. Unfortunately, that was a route Cobain – a victim of rock's style wars as much as the next enthusiast – denied himself.

A 'star' in the eyes of the world, he never lost sight of the essential worthlessness that lay at the heart of the human condition. In five years, he could be forgotten, in one hundred years' time, the world would (nuclear war notwithstanding) be populated by an entirely different set of people. This cycle of impermanence was expressed in the song's final mantra, "All in all is all we are", which sounded like a cast-off from an old Quintessence album.

Inviting Scott Litt to remix the track hinted not only at its commercial potential. While no 'Teen Spirit', the song was more radio-friendly than much else on the record, and there was a suspicion that Steve Albini wasn't the man to bring out the best in this most delicate song on the album, a fragility accentuated by Kera Schaley's simple cello line.

Recording artists often like to reserve their most poignant songs for the end of their albums, and Cobain was no different than Jagger and Richards, Eddie Vedder or Marc Bolan in that respect. Even ignoring the lyrics, which took an almost nonchalant perspective on self-hatred, it was obvious that 'All Apologies' had special meaning for Cobain. He wrote it early in 1992, around the same time as 'Heart-Shaped Box', by which time his marriage with Courtney Love seemed to threaten the very existence of the band. It was also the song he chose to dedicate to his wife and newborn daughter at the band's legendary August 1992 Reading Festival appearance. Sinead O'Connor later covered the song on her *Universal Mother* album.

GALLONS OF RUBBING ALCOHOL FLOW THROUGH THE STRIP

TUCKING away a 'secret' track onto the end of CDs might have been fun first time around, and 'Endless, Nameless' probably made the wait worthwhile on *Nevermind*. but with nothing much to subvert on the more abrasive *In Utero*, 'Gallons Of Rubbing Alcohol Flow Through The Strip', which cut in some twenty minutes after the end of 'All Apologies', was an anti-climax, a freely-associating jam around the bare scraps of a musical idea. The fold-out sleeve described it as a "Devalued American Dollar Purchase Incentive Track"; the lyrics were replaced by one word: "Whatever", which showed just how much effort went into the piece.

COMPILATIONS

THUS FAR, THE NIRVANA CATALOGUE HAS BEEN RELATIVELY STRAIGHTFORWARD. The band forms in the late Eighties, and gets picked up by a local indie label that releases their debut album. Poached by a major, the group celebrate with a record that's destined to figure in Top 100 Album polls for as long as rock survives. With an attitude to their new-found celebrity that fluctuates from the merely playful to the bitterly contemptuous, Nirvana's third record emerges carrying a placard marked "uncompromising". It wasn't half as scary as it might have been, but Kurt Cobain's suicide the following year certainly was, prompting a huge debate on the relationship between rock and art, and art and life.

Meanwhile, after a short respite, which saw both Geffen and Sub Pop exercising commercial restraint, more Nirvana product inevitably followed. As will become clear later on in this section, there is still plenty of scope to 'tidy up' the many odds-and-sods in the band's catalogue. Such ordering would have been anathema to Cobain's instincts, of course – look no further than *Incesticide*, the only compilation issued during his lifetime for evidence of his intemperate attitude towards the band's past work...

Incesticide

Geffen GEF 24504; December 1992

WITH *NEVERMIND* STILL SELLING STRONGLY, ASSISTED BY THE FOUR SINGLES lifted from it, issuing a follow-up during 1992 would not have made good commercial sense. Sad, but that's the way the big-time record industry works, and Nirvana were by this time a very big part of that game.

A compromise option was to pull together some of the loose ends from the band's back catalogue for a 'new' album of 'collector's cuts'. Without a huge promotional fanfare, it was clearly aimed at the enthusiast, but if passing trade chanced upon it, then all well and good.

The result was *Incesticide*, a kind of belated prequel to *Nevermind* that was useful to the band if only to provide further ammunition for their increasingly non-corporate behaviour. It also kept the record companies happy. (Though issued by Geffen, the set was put together in conjunction with Sub Pop, who controlled much of the material.) Some time earlier, the Seattle label was preparing to go alone with a 'Rarities' package, provisionally titled *Cash Cow*, but the proliferation of Nirvana bootlegs on the market helped foster a mood of collaboration.

Although a retrospective wasn't quite the same thing as an album of brand-new material, anything bearing the name of the most talked-about international band of '92 was going to be something of an event. But when the furore over Cobain's original sleeve-notes threatened to upstage the record, it was evidence enough that the Kurt'n'Courtney soap opera was getting out of hand.

It was a perfect example of the contradictory impulses that propelled the Cobain dynamic. On the one hand, Kurt castigated his enemies – Lynn Hirschberg, who wrote the unflattering portrait of Courtney Love in *Vanity Fair*; those who still suspected his wife was the uncrowned Gold-Digger Of '92; the 'Polly' rapists; and the racists, homophobes and misogynists who called themselves Nirvana fans, at whom he railed: "Leave us the fuck alone! Don't come to our shows and don't buy our records". On the other, wearing his benevolent, cheerleading head, Kurt used the note to express his slavish devotion to other rock bands: cult names like the late Seventies all-women avant-punkers The Raincoats, American maverick Daniel Johnston, The Melvins, Shonen Knife, The Jesus Lizard, Sonic Youth, The Breeders and Hole.

Cobain had little to write about his own group, but when he did, it was typically self-deprecating: "I'll be the first to admit that we're the Nineties version of Cheap Trick or The Knack, but the last to admit that it hasn't been rewarding." Although widely published at the time, Cobain's original note never made it to the CD issue, which, apart from the bare minimum of details about each song, is most notable for his drawing of a mutant baby clutching a skeleton, which in turn is caressing a rose. The Cobain family, perhaps?

DIVE

(Cobain/Novoselic)

'D IVE' WAS the first fruit of Nirvana's April 1990 session with producer Butch Vig in Smart Studios. Issued in September 1990 as the flip to 'Sliver', the band's last full 45 for Sub Pop, it seemed to distil all that was best about the *Bleach* material into three minutes. 'Dive' was almost stereotypically 'grunge' – powerful blue collar rhythms that veered towards clumsiness, and a metal-friendly voice that roared Plant-like with an added layer of punkish menace.

Chad Channing proved himself a solid skinsman without displaying any of the imaginative flourishes Dave Grohl later brought to the band. The chorus, a slow, determined ascent up the fretboard, was a neat inversion of the song's downwardly-inclined 'dive' hook. By 1990, the song was regarded as one of the band's best.

'Dive' had first been recorded in June 1989, at a session taped at the

Evergreen State College in Olympia, where Bruce Pavitt had launched his 'Subterranean Pop' fanzine a decade earlier. At this stage, the song was known as 'Down With Me', and while that particular version was shelved, another song taped that day, a version of Kiss's 'Do You Love Me', later found its way onto a compilation. It was the only official evidence that second guitarist Jason Everman was ever in the band.

SLIVER
(Cobain/Novoselic)

Dan PETERS, the Mudhoney drummer who went on to hold the fort briefly for The Screaming Trees, was a Nirvana member for an even shorter length of time – but long enough to play at the groundbreaking Seattle's Motor Sports International show, in September 1990, and to record the band's second A-side two months earlier, on July 11.

Even that was all over in an hour, because the band had sneaked a session with Jack Endino while Tad were on a lunch-break from recording. The band's frontman Tad Doyle wasn't too keen on the notorious equipment wreckers from Aberdeen wreaking havoc on his gear, so Endino had to ensure order was maintained during the session. Not that there was much time for such antics. But leaving aside the oddly-recorded bassline, the down-to-business approach had no real adverse effects: the in-yer-face dynamics of 'Sliver' enhanced the band's international reputation tenfold – despite the fact that only 3,000 copies were manufactured in the States and just 2,000 in the UK, all on coloured vinyl.

Though instantly cherished by the band's growing audience, 'Sliver' was, in Cobain's eyes, "the most ridiculous pop song that I had ever written". It was dashed off in about an hour, and the reason it had to be recorded as soon as an opportunity presented itself was because Peters was about to be called back into the Mudhoney fold. Lyrically, it was one of the most significant of Cobain's early songs, a slice of autobiography about being farmed out to his grandparents while his parents enjoyed a night out. The urgency of the "Grandma take me home" chorus emphasises Cobain's fraught relationship with his grandfather, a man who apparently looked like the old Soviet Union leader Brezhnev, and was in Cobain's assessment "a dick".

The single version differs to the slightly edited one here in that a snippet of conversation between Jonathan Poneman and a hungover Krist Novoselic, culled from the bassist's answering machine, cuts in at the end of the track. Cobain was particularly proud of the title, delighting in the knowledge that people would inevitably call it 'Silver'.

STAIN
(Cobain/Novoselic)

THE GLORIOUS lack of sophistication of the *Bleach* material wasn't immediately jettisoned by the band: 'Stain' motors on a single riff, and contains just one verse of contemptuous self-hate repeated three times. What had changed was Nirvana's ambitions in the studio, which is why they opted to record it with Steve Fisk, a veteran of various sessions with local bands, at the 24-track Music Source Studios on Seattle's Capitol Hill.

Cobain apparently told Fisk that, "We need a Top Forty drum sound", and the results suggest that more effort went into achieving that than anything else. The drums are right upfront in the mix alongside Cobain's vocals; only during the break does his guitar become anything other than a passenger.

The Fisk session took place in September 1989, by which time *Bleach* had been out for several weeks and second guitarist Jason Everman had already left. Also taped at Music Source were three tracks that have yet to appear officially: 'Even In His Youth', 'Token Eastern Song' and an electric version of 'Polly', later reworked for *Nevermind*. A fifth song, 'Been A Son', joined 'Stain' on the 'Blew' EP, which was issued on Sub Pop's Tupelo subsidiary, together with 'Love Buzz' and the title track.

BEEN A SON
(Cobain/Novoselic)

CONFUSINGLY, this isn't the Steve Fisk-recorded version of 'Been A Son', which joined 'Stain' on the 'Blew' 12". That was passed up for a take recorded for BBC Radio 1 over two years later, on November 9, 1991, during the band's European visit to promote 'Smells Like Teen Spirit' and *Nevermind*. It was broadcast on the *Mark Goodier Show*, Nirvana's fourth session for the UK radio station, on November 18. That day's version of 'Something In The Way' was the session's only track not to make it onto *Incesticide*.

'Been A Son' may have dated back to 1989, but its subject matter (the generally unstated cultural preference for sons over daughters) and the instantly uplifting, Beatlesque style, complete with Dave Grohl harmonies, made it a perfect promotional tool just as the band was reaching towards a wider audience. Even the break, usually an excuse for some impassioned Cobain soloing, was a model of restraint.

TURNAROUND
(Mark Mothersbaugh/ Gerald Casale)

THE MOST influential DJ in Britain, and quite possibly the planet, is John Peel. He'd already profiled the band, and the emerging Seattle scene, for the national Sunday broadsheet *The Observer* back in 1989, and it was inevitable that Nirvana would pay him a visit on their early trips to London.

While nothing from the band's first Peel session (November 1989) has been officially released, three of the four songs from the second, taped a year later, were retrieved for this retrospective, by way of the *Hormoaning* mini-album, issued late in 1991 to coincide with dates in Australia and Japan. (The 'missing' number was 'D-7'.) The session had some special significance: it marked the recording debut of Dave Grohl with Nirvana.

It was also notable for its song selection – instead of promoting their own work, three of the four tracks were covers. 'Turnaround' was an early cut by Devo, one of the few American responses to punk to make an impact in the hotly divided UK. Despite the song's robotic, staccato style, Nirvana made an effective translation, which was helped by Cobain's convincing vocal performance. Lyrically, the paranoia and misanthropism in 'Turnaround' seemed to fit the Nirvana *oeuvre* perfectly.

MOLLY'S LIPS
(Eugene Kelly/Frances McKee)

THE REMAINING two cover versions taped for John Peel's programme were even more obscure. Both songs were originally issued on short-run 45s by Edinburgh-based duo The Vaselines, who enjoyed a

fleeting glimpse of the indie sector spotlight during the late Eighties before splitting. Revelling in his esoteric tastes (which he copped from K Records supremo Calvin Johnson), Cobain told Gina Arnold in 1992 that The Vaselines were his "favourite band ever... They didn't even influence me, it was just a reminder of how much I really value innocence and children and my youth."

He was less pleased when an earlier version of 'Molly's Lips' became a *bona fide* part of the Nirvana catalogue shortly before the band's imminent departure from Sub Pop. As a condition of leaving, Sub Pop were promised one further single. Cobain was reluctant to waste one of his new songs, and so an earlier studio recording of 'Molly's Lips', featuring Chad Channing on drums, was issued, back-to-back with a track by the Fluid.

SON OF A GUN
(Eugene Kelly/Frances McKee)

IT'S A MINOR quirk of the Eighties UK indie scene that The Vaselines never recorded a session for John Peel. However, this belated exposure prompted the group to reform for a performance at a Nirvana concert in Edinburgh in the winter of 1990. Within two years, the hitherto little-known Scottish duo even had their own Sub Pop compilation, *The Way Of*.

'Son Of A Gun', which is often confused by fans with 'Turnaround' because of its "Turn-turn-turn around" refrain, brought out the pop singer in Cobain, his voice sounding uncharacteristically stylised and trouble-free. It was the incorporation of cover versions like these which began to tip the scales of Nirvana's influences from metal and hard rock to the more marginal climes of the punk-inspired DIY movement – ironically, at a time when the band was about to shed its own indie status.

(NEW WAVE) POLLY

Another track recorded in November 1991 for the *Mark Goodier Show* on BBC's Radio 1, '(New Wave) Polly' was a fast and frivolous reworking of the *Nevermind* track, hence its '(New Wave)' prefix. Frivolous in retrospect, that is, only after Butch Vig had encouraged Cobain to perform the song acoustically at the Smart session. Before then, Nirvana had been hammering out 'Polly' in electrifying punk rock fashion. There was no question about which version proved most effective, but this Buzzcocks-inspired rendition became the session's major talking-point.

Despite its early origins, Dave Grohl (who puts in a splendid performance) received a composer credit alongside Cobain and Novoselic on the album sleeve. These are not to be trusted: Nirvana songbooks rightly credit Cobain as sole composer.

BEESWAX

NIRVANA's early blend of hardcore and hard rock rarely yielded a more grizzled hybrid than 'Beeswax'. Recorded at the January 1988 demo session at Reciprocal with producer Jack Endino, it produced a searing vocal from Cobain, a characteristically heavyweight performance out of drummer Dale Crover, and a head-against-the-wall treatment from the band as a whole.

On the face of it, Cobain's vocal is a blend of Big Black frontman Steve Albini's against-the-beat, barely-decipherable monologue style, and Scratch Acid's David Yow's end-of-tether yell. Midway through, a stray phrase concerning "cotton candy" reveals another, far more surprising source of inspiration: Antennae Jimmy Semens' extraordinary 'rap' on 'Pena', a track on Captain Beefheart's legendary *Trout Mask Replica* album – which Cobain reportedly played frequently during the winter of 1990. On this evidence, he probably encountered the record much earlier.

'Beeswax' introduces the latter part of the CD, which concentrates on material drawn from Nirvana's pre-fame days. The earliest documentation of this particular song dates from practice sessions early in 1987. Prior to its appearance on *Incesticide*, 'Beeswax' first turned up on the *Kill Rock Stars* compilation (KRS 201), issued to launch the label of the same name. The album was released in August 1991, just in time for the International Pop Underground Convention in Olympia, organised by Calvin Johnson's K label. A manifesto produced for the event bore the legend: "No lackeys to the corporate ogre allowed". *Nevermind* was released three weeks later.

DOWNER
(Cobain/Novoselic)

THIS IS THE same Jack Endino-produced version that appears on the *Bleach* CD. Refer back to that entry for further explication.

MEXICAN SEAFOOD

WHAT BEGINS as a pesky little new wave number quickly descends into a heavily accented pre-grunge sound, with Cobain cataloguing various skin complaints. The link between that and the song's title is that seafood can often cause skin irritations to flare up, though one commentator, Chuck Crisafulli, suggests that the song refers to a regretted sexual encounter.

'Mexican Seafood' was being performed as far back as early 1987, when it was one of several songs that featured in Nirvana's broadcast on Olympia's alternative radio station, KAOS, in April. It formed part of the set taped by Jack Endino at

Reciprocal in January 1988, and had the local C/Z label got its finger out, could have been the first Nirvana track to make it onto vinyl. Sub Pop beat them to it, but the track did eventually surface on the limited edition *Teriyaki Asthma Vol. 1* EP (C/Z CZ 009) in November 1989.

HAIRSPRAY QUEEN

A NEAT FUSION of UK art-punk, as epitomised by the Gang Of Four-like bassline; and America's primal hardcore scene, witness Cobain's Scratch Acid-type yowls. Throw in some genre-busting guitar – from staccato Steppenwolf to Thurston Moore-like waywardness in seconds – and you have the early Nirvana in a nutshell, struggling to free themselves from the sum of their influences. That said, 'Hairspray Queen', another hangover from early 1987, already revealed Cobain's penchant for interrupting the mood of the song: its chorus hung sweetly on a single chord in complete contrast to the busy verses.

This recording dates from the January 1988 Reciprocal Studios session with Jack Endino, and later prompted Cobain to quip, "How New Wave we were".

AERO ZEPPELIN
(Cobain/Novoselic)

NOT ONE of the band's more impressive song titles, as Cobain later admitted: "Christ! Let's just throw together some heavy metal riffs in no particular order and give it a quirky name in homage to a couple of our favourite masturbatory Seventies rock acts." The lyric, a commentary (though that's probably overstating it a bit) on fandom, with particular reference to dinosaur bands, is equally forgettable.

The track itself, another early number from Nirvana's 1987 set later recorded with Jack Endino in 1988, was far more interesting. It started out, somewhat inconceivably, like an early Scritti Politti outtake – trebly guitar, fractured rhythm, even a voice that at times sounded remarkably like Scritti frontman Green. As if to further pile on the evidence that the early Nirvana didn't quite know into which direction to go, the track soon develops into a mighty exercise in riffery, gifting Cobain with another opportunity to flex his atonal-style soloing muscles. Even drummer Dale Crover makes himself heard even more than usual on a song that isn't likely to endear itself to enthusiasts of *Nevermind*.

BIG LONG NOW
(Cobain/Novoselic)

PART OF the explanation behind Jason Everman's departure in the summer of 1989 was that he preferred ponderous, dirge-like material like 'Big Long Now' to Cobain's increasingly pop-friendly tastes. That does the song a disservice. True, it is ponderous, slow and punishing like the worst kind of torture. And it's long, clocking in at over five minutes. But for all its Melvins-inspired procrastination, 'Big Long Now' is rescued majestically by Cobain during the chorus, the tension in his searching yell saying as much as his words ever could. It's easy to see why this Jack Endino production didn't make it onto *Bleach*, and why it was buried in the running-order for *Incesticide*, but 'Big Long Now' is still capable of leaving a more lasting impression than some of the more characteristic Nirvana songs.

ANEURYSM
(Cobain/Novoselic/Grohl)

COMMERCIALLY speaking, the last half of *Incesticide* had nosedived into the bewildering mire of Nirvana's earliest work. It bade farewell, though, in more friendly fashion, with this classic crossover track. 'Aneurysm' warms up on a deceptive, *Bleach*-era riff, before Cobain makes his peace with pop ("Come on over and do the Twist!"), and a real song emerges, with all the instrumental space and vocal harmonies of *Nevermind*.

Taking its title from a blood-related complaint, 'Aneurysm' couched Cobain's penchant for self-flagellation (its "beat me out of me" chorus being a classic Cobainism) within the context of drug use. The resulting musical high emphasised its show of catharsis, which quickly made the song a regular in Nirvana's live set.

'Aneurysm' was the third track culled from the session recorded for Radio 1's *Mark Goodier Show*, in November 1991, though an earlier version had already appeared on the *Hormoaning* EP (see separate entry).

Unplugged In New York

Geffen GED 24727, October 1994

MTV'S *UNPLUGGED* SERIES WAS A SMART MOVE BY THE TELEVISION STATION that tempted international stars into its studio, thus boosting its profile among older viewers, who in turn brought in major advertisers tempted by the opportunity to reach a market with far more spending power than teenagers and students. Offering major players like Eric Clapton, Rod Stewart and Paul McCartney the chance to show off their musical skills in an acoustic setting, *Unplugged* inadvertently handed them a lifeline. Away from studios where they'd invariably be convinced by cloth-eared engineers that hi-tech was where it's at, these rock'n'roll dinosaurs could present their songs in a more sympathetic – and rarefied – atmosphere, where godawful Eighties production values were banished in favour of a more 'authentic' musical presentation.

When Nirvana were invited to perform for the MTV cameras, at Sony Studios on November 18, 1993, two months after the release of *In Utero*, the process worked in reverse. Here was a band whose reputation had been founded on the powers of (a sometimes sanitised) hardcore, being given the opportunity to reveal another side to their work.

Few in the Nirvana camp doubted the quality of Cobain's songwriting, although having spent the past five years camouflaged by electricity of some kind or another, there was some concern over whether the band's technical limitations would be exposed by the professionally intimate setting and crystal-clear sound. They needn't have worried: any reservations (and shock at seeing the band so static) were quickly dispelled by a spellbinding performance that revealed Cobain as a passionate and accomplished writer, and a charismatic and intense frontman.

The arrangements worked well too, with Krist Novoselic wielding an acoustic bass, and Dave Grohl managing to curb his wildest John Bonham fantasies. Veteran hardcore guitarist Pat Smear (ex-Germs), who'd joined the band in time for their American leg of the *In Utero* tour, helped flesh out the sound, as did cellist Lori Goldston, from Seattle's Black Cat Orchestra.

Just three songs were 'unplugged' from *In Utero*, with the remainder culled either from the Nirvana back catalogue, or from an imaginative selection of half-a-dozen cover versions. Orchids and burning candles lit the stage, creating a mood of intimacy that was in direct contrast to the standard Nirvana live show. An element of conviviality was ensured when Cobain invited Meat Puppets Curt and Cris Kirkwood on stage to collaborate on three of their own songs, another in a long line of Kurt's 'cheerleading' gestures.

The *Unplugged* show was produced by the band in conjunction with Scott Litt, and was bootlegged almost immediately after it had been broadcast. Four months later Cobain took his own life, shooting himself in the head on April 5, 1994. When the CD appeared officially, in October 1994, it served as an effective and emotional tribute to Cobain, the acoustic setting in some way enhancing the sense that this was a window on the private Kurt. Two tracks not featured on the original broadcast were added to the CD edition.

ABOUT A GIRL

"THIS IS OFF our first record. Most people don't own it," said Cobain by way of introduction. 'About A Girl' was the earliest Nirvana song in the *Unplugged* set, though its selection as the opening song wasn't down to chronology. Its effortlessly simple structure, plus the fact that the Cobain/Novoselic/Grohl line-up had been performing it for over three years, made it a perfect choice to settle any nerves. The chord changes were hardly going to trouble newcomer Pat Smear, while Dave Grohl, brushes in hand, managed not to exceed the required featherlight touch. Not much could go wrong – Cobain opted to keep his break simple and succinct – and not much did.

COME AS YOU ARE

THE FIRST OF Nirvana's soft/hard songs to get the pared-down treatment, this too lost very little in translation, with Cobain employing a chorus effect pedal to capture the submerged guitar sound of the *Nevermind* version. The meaning of the song, most acutely the line, "And I swear that I don't have a gun", had altered dramatically by the time the CD appeared, just months after Cobain's suicide.

JESUS DOESN'T WANT ME FOR A SUNBEAM
(Eugene Kelly/Francis McKee)

SCOTTISH DUO The Vaselines had previously arranged this old Christian song, which (as 'Jesus Wants Me For A Sunbeam') was best-known as a school assembly favourite when an alternative to 'He's Got The Whole World In His Hands' was required. Novoselic switched from bass to squeeze-box for the number and emphasised the song's origins as standard fare for itinerant preachers armed only with a portable harmonium.

Nirvana had been performing 'Jesus... ' intermittently ever since 1991 (a version turns up on a bootleg recorded at the Astoria late that year, for example), and its evocation of an infants-eye-view to music was especially poignant to Cobain. Even more crucial was the complete change of emphasis given to the song by The Vaselines, who stood its oppressively God-friendly lyric on its head. It was perfect for the singer whose sense of self-hate was so great that even the all-welcoming Jesus Christ rejects him.

THE MAN WHO SOLD THE WORLD
(David Bowie)

CONTROL, selling, a man's relationship with the world, death – suddenly, this seemingly unlikely cover version begins to make sense. David Bowie first released the song in 1971 on the album of the same name, adorned (in the UK at least) with a sleeve that depicted the soon-to-be glam icon reclining in a satin dress. Despite Bowie's glam reputation, both his cross-dressing and his discomfort with the world around him obviously appealed to Cobain. This version, which produced audible gasps amongst the audience as recognition set in, remained remarkably faithful to the original, though Cobain's subtle fuzz guitar lead (which gave the song a different ending) and the introduction of a stray minor chord into the arrangement elevated the treatment beyond pale replication. Cobain may have fulfilled many of his ominous off-the-cuff remarks, but the one that preceded this song ("I guarantee you I'll screw this song up") wasn't one of them.

PENNYROYAL TEA

COBAIN struggled to reach the high notes in this, the latest fan favourite in the short but explosive Nirvana canon, but such technical shortcomings only served to enhance the song's barely concealed mood of desperation. That Cobain chose to perform the song alone with his guitar added to the poignancy, although his "Am I gonna do this one by myself?" quip wasn't quite convincing in its bid to convey spontaneity.

DUMB

WITH Lori Goldston replicating Kera Schaley's cello part, this version remained faithful to the *In Utero* original, which was one of that album's more Spartan songs and an obvious choice for the show. Dave Grohl contributed backing vocals, though it was Cobain's at-times detached presence during the performance that seemed to wring an extra pound of irony from the words "think I'm just happy".

POLLY

NIRVANA concerts were usually boisterous affairs, an excuse to get pasted to a high-octane soundtrack that was always more joyous exorcism than a collective sharing of grief – in spite of all the 'loser' associations. 'Polly' proved an exception to that, often providing an "Unplugged" element to the band's shows.

In the television studio, where the band's music was stripped of all its headbanging qualities, there was no escape from the down-at-mouth thesis that ran through Cobain's work. Coming off the back of two strongly downbeat songs, the brutal irony of 'Polly' threatened to transform the show into a lament on the beastliness of the human condition – except for the fact that the song's melody, augmented by Grohl's impressive harmonies, could hardly have been sweeter.

ON A PLAIN

THE BAND returned for this, an in-concert favourite from the second side of *Nevermind*, which breathed some inoffensive pop values back into the performance. That is, if you don't take the portentous "One more special message to go/And then I'm done, and then I can go home" line too seriously. There was a subtle lyric change, too: mindful, perhaps, that his mother was in the audience, Cobain substituted "brother" for "mother" in the line, "My mother died every night".

SOMETHING IN THE WAY

THE INTIMACY captured by Vig as he recorded the song at the *Nevermind* sessions was easy to replicate in the *Unplugged* environment. The entrance of the rhythm section during the choruses lent the song a heavy heartbeat, which was tempered by Lori Goldston's simple, mournful cello line.

PLATEAU
OH ME
LAKE OF FIRE
(all Curt Kirkwood)

BROTHERS Curt and Cris Kirkwood of The Meat Puppets, were visibly bemused as they ambled onto Nirvana's much-awaited *Unplugged* stage, invited (as they were for the recent *In Utero* tour) by Cobain in one of his frequent magnanimous gestures. Kurt's support for all manner of left-field, small-scale indie bands wasn't merely benevolence. By namechecking bands like The Vaselines, The Raincoats, The Wipers and The Meat Puppets, Cobain was reacquainting himself with the feelings of fanworship he first experienced as a teenager back in Aberdeen, a reminder of more innocent times when all that was at stake was a class reputation. Now, when Cobain scrawled the name of one of his musical passions (invariably drawn from the dustier backwaters of rock history), he knew that critics would rush off to write retrospectives, and that many Nirvana fans would follow up his recommendations. That, to Cobain, was one of the most positive and enriching aspects of stardom.

The Meat Puppets, who hailed from Phoenix, Arizona, had persevered with their rootsy brand of hardcore – always melodic, often wilfully quirky – for a decade without ever troubling chart compilers. Even on the American alternative circuit, the band never assumed the kind of passionate fan-following enjoyed by contemporaries like Dinosaur Jr or Big Black. So Cobain's patronage was all the more surprising, offering the Meat Puppets an international platform that they'd long given up all hope of achieving.

'Plateau', the first of the three songs, was as melancholy as any Nirvana song, though unlike anything written by Cobain, it seemed to have more in common with a pre-pop sensibility. So did the lyric, which despite the song's sea-shanty rhythm, sounded like a mystical take on environmentalism. Surprisingly, bearing in mind he'd invited the band along and no doubt had a firm hand on the material, Cobain swivels on his chair as if he's bored by the proceedings. Either that, or he's covering up for the fact that he's without a guitar and therefore propless and naked.

'Oh Me' was again culled from Cobain's favourite Meat Puppets album, *Meat Puppets II*, issued in 1983, and was far more accomplished, both in interpretation and performance, than the ragged 'Plateau'. Pity, then, that this was one of two songs that never made it on to the original Unplugged broadcast.

'Lake Of Fire' found Cobain once again struggling to reach The Meat Puppets' upper registers, though there was an intensity about his efforts that was not heard on the previous two cuts. The song's country-tinged feel seemed to offer an alternative meaning for all those flannel shirts favoured by the Seattle bands. Here was someone, apparently rootless and adrift from the society in which he found himself, reacquainting himself with the traditions of American music through a maverick and fiercely independent alternative band. Like another Seattle musical legend, Jimi Hendrix, who had rediscovered his black music roots shortly before his death, Cobain had little time to develop this *rapprochement* with the past.

ALL APOLOGIES

THIS REMAINS one of the most important songs in the Nirvana canon, not least because the lyrics read uncannily like a suicide-note. It was only a matter of weeks after the *Unplugged* broadcast that Cobain was moved to write a longer one – this time for real.

As with 'Dumb', the band had little trouble translating this into the *Unplugged* format, especially with Lori Goldston on hand to play out yet another simple, affecting cello line. Cobain did make one subtle lyric change, so that the mantra-like coda now became "All alone is all we are". You couldn't have wished for a more poignant ending – but that didn't reckon with the one final ace Cobain had up his sleeve.

WHERE DID YOU SLEEP LAST NIGHT
(Leadbelly, alias Huddie Ledbetter)

IF THERE was one performance Cobain intended his audience to take away with them from *Unplugged*, it would be this, the most intriguing and convincing cover in the entire set. As the show unfolded, the Bowie, the Vaselines and the Meat Puppets songs were either introduced, or else needed little introduction. Not so this mantra-like incantation, culled from the repertoire of legendary bluesman Leadbelly, and later sanitised (as 'Black Girl') for pop audiences by the Four Pennies, who enjoyed a Top Twenty hit with it in 1964.

While the electric buzz thrill of Nirvana's music could often mask the desperation at the core of Cobain's writing, it took another man's song, hauled in from another era and played in another style, to provide the show with its unexpected and breathtaking finale. In terms of rock exorcisms, it ranked alongside John Lennon's 1970 *Plastic Ono Band* album.

Although immersed in rock and pop values, the driving force behind Cobain's work was little different to that which had fuelled the greatest recording artists this century. White males, even those hailing from a backwater like Aberdeen, weren't necessarily the most put-upon section of American society, but Cobain's estrangement from mainstream values was no less significant than the racial hatred and poverty that informed the early development of the blues. In some ways, it might even have been worse: his acute misanthropy robbed him even of the mild palliative of collective suffering.

This affinity with Leadbelly, a singer noted for his primitive yet powerful style, was not something Cobain had lately developed. He originally borrowed a copy of the *Leadbelly's Last Sessions* double-album from his next door neighbour, one Slim Moon, back in 1988. Word is that Kurt's interest was first aroused after he read a quote from veteran Beat writer William Burroughs saying that Leadbelly is where you go if you want to hear real passion in music. Within weeks, he'd sought out other Leadbelly recordings, and photographs of the bluesman started appearing on his walls. Cobain was unequivocal when he explained his fascination to biographer Michael Azerrad: "It's so raw and sincere. It's something that I hold really sacred to me. Leadbelly is one of the most important things in my life. I'm totally obsessed with him."

Shortly after the release of *Bleach*, in August 1989, Cobain sat in on sessions for The Screaming Trees' Mark Lanegan's solo album. They collaborated on two Leadbelly songs, though only one ended up on the eventual album, *The Winding Sheet* (Sub Pop SP 61B, 1990). That song was 'Where Did You Sleep Last Night', with Kurt Cobain on lead guitar and Krist Novoselic on bass. (The discarded cut, which featured Cobain on vocals, was 'Ain't It A Shame'.) The sessions went so well that the Nirvana frontman apparently toyed with the idea of forming an occasional blues band, for which he suggested the name Lithium.

The image of one man, his guitar and a headful of tunes wrenched from the pit of his heart is an enduring one. Though Cobain found the powers of punk/metal noise irresistible, he rarely lost sight of the relationship between spirituality and music, a lesson he'd picked up from Leadbelly. This stunning performance introduced the folk-blues hero to yet another generation, while Cobain breathed meaning into what on the face of it appears to be a simple song of infidelity, but on closer inspection yields greater metaphorical delights.

So memorable was the performance that months before the *Unplugged* show appeared on CD, Geffen and the band were considering issuing this version as the flip-side to 'Pennyroyal Tea', the projected follow-up single to 'All Apologies'. Courtney Love's band Hole got there first, performing the song by way of a tribute to Cobain when they returned to Seattle for a show on September 11, 1994.

From The Muddy Banks Of The Wishkah

Geffen GED 25105, October 1996

SINCE NIRVANA'S DEMISE, DAVE GROHL AND KRIST NOVOSELIC HAVE BEEN consulted on all the band's posthumous releases. Although rifts with Cobain's estate – namely Courtney Love – have been the source of much media speculation, it seems unlikely that a situation will ensue that is comparable with that endured by Experience members Noel Redding and Mitch Mitchell after the death of Jimi Hendrix.

Grohl and Novoselic were first put to work on a 'tribute' live collection back in summer 1994, but both pulled out claiming – understandably, given the circumstances – "emotional drag". What was intended to be a 35-song double live set, titled *Verse, Chorus, Verse*, was dropped in favour of a simple *Unplugged* CD, and the *Live! Tonight! Sold Out!* video, which was being compiled at the time of Cobain's death.

A shortened version of the live album eventually appeared in October 1996. Its arrival coincided with Britpop fatigue in the UK, which allowed critics to see beyond feel-good, Sixties-derived pop anthems and once again, proclaim Nirvana as the most important band of the Nineties. The band didn't only signify the last gasp of Rock Romanticism. Nirvana's arrival and soaraway success allowed rock to wash its hands of the hi-tech production techniques of the previous decade, so much so that even dinosaur bands like The Rolling Stones (always eager to spot prevailing trends) began to dirty up their sound. Even in death, Cobain's influence was obvious – all the searching, and the possibility that rock's celebratory sound might be inextricably linked with death drives, caused a flight from excess and passion into the safety of craftmanship and career-building that were the foundation-stones of Britpop.

Even Krist Novoselic, who'd been forced to confront much more than most of us could ever imagine, was keen to free himself from the questions and enjoy the band's music for what it was. In his otherwise perfunctory sleeve-note for this collection, he concluded: "Let all the analysis fall away like yellow, aged newsprint. Crank this record up and realise the bliss, power and passion... TOTAL NIRVANA!"

It was on stage that this passion was most keenly felt, not only by the fans but by the group themselves. For Cobain, a sensualist for whom living was a series of emotional highs and lows, gigs were the front-line of the Nirvana experience. In his suicide-note, he made several references to his inability to believe in his music anymore, most of these referring specifically to the concert situation. The physicality that he brought to his performances had become the tricks of a trained circus animal.

In the final moments of his life, Cobain wrote: "When we were backstage and the lights go out and the manic roar of the crowd begins, it doesn't affect me the way in which it did for Freddy (*sic*) Mercury, who seemed to love and relish on the love and adoration from the crowd – which is something I totally admire and envy." Despite the favourable financial statements that would arrive at his door, and the regular meetings with the suits, Cobain was never at ease in the entertainment business. Long-in-the-tooth rock watchers could easily forget that fact – how many musicians have got high on rebellion before settling for respectability?

Cobain, who used rock as his confession-box, as his confidante, still found this potentially intense art-form unequal to the test of maintaining his interest in life itself. His note continued: "The fact is, I can't fool you. Any one of you. It simply isn't fair to you or me. The worst crime I can think of would be to rip people off by faking in and pretending as if I'm having 100% fun. Sometimes I feel as if I should have a punch-in time clock before I walk out on stage." His last words hammered the sentiments home: "I don't have the passion anymore and so remember, it's better to burn out than to fade away."

INTRO

BEFORE Cobain's suicide, the sense of anguish that underpinned his music was counterbalanced by the pleasures of its cathartic celebration. Once he was gone, it was impossible to listen the band's music in quite the same way again. Cobain's final actions had breathed real life into a rock art form that had become largely gestural and symbolic.

When *From The Muddy Banks Of The Wishkah* began with just under a minute's-worth of Cobain shrieking uncontrollably, it was as if to say that this, in essence, was what he was trying to say. The pop melodies, the hard rock beat, the punkish attitude, all of these were merely recognisable vehicles for the wordless rage that Cobain felt "in the pit of my nauseous stomach".

SCHOOL

THIS *Bleach*-era number was filmed and recorded by VPRO-TV at the Paradiso, Amsterdam, for broadcast on Dutch TV. The show took place on November 25, 1991, during Nirvana's second European tour that year.

DRAIN YOU

THIS VERSION of the *Nevermind* favourite was taped by the syndicated radio broadcasters Westwood One at Del Mar Fairgrounds, just outside San Diego, California, on December 28, 1991. It was the second show of a brief tour of the West Coast, where the rapidly ascending Nirvana were booked on a bill with Pearl Jam and headliners Red Hot Chili Peppers. According to Krist Novoselic, the band was in an aggressive mood that evening, resulting in a particularly feisty performance.

ANEURYSM

THIS VERSION of the 'Teen Spirit' B-side was recorded at the Del Mar Fairgrounds show in late December 1991, almost exactly a year after it had been recorded in a studio.

SMELLS LIKE TEEN SPIRIT

IT HAD only been out on single a couple of months, but already Nirvana were taking 'Teen Spirit' at a faster pace than originally intended. Once again, this came from the Del Mar Fairgrounds show.

BEEN A SON

A TREBLE-HEAVY sound quality doesn't impair the performance of this lesser-known track, originally issued on the pre-Geffen *Blew* EP. This version of 'Been A Son' came from the November 25, 1991 Paradiso show in Amsterdam.

LITHIUM

BEFORE it was afforded single status, 'Lithium' wasn't the mass audience singalong it later became. This version, culled from the Amsterdam Paradiso broadcast, was far more powerful, with just one rasping voice at the helm.

SLIVER

THIS, ONE of the oldest songs in the 1993 set, was taped midway through Nirvana's final US tour, at the Civic Center, Springfield, Massachusetts, on November 10, 1993. Even when Cobain affected boredom when delivering his over-familiar material, it was accepted as integral to, rather than detracting from, the overall performance. By this time, Pat Smear was in the group, on second guitar and backing vocals.

SPANK THRU

THIS WAS the second live version of 'Spank Thru' to gain official release (the first appeared on the UK 'Sliver' 12"/CD, issued in 1991). This particular version was taped by Stereoral at Il Castello Vi De Porta, Castello 41, Rome, Italy, on November 19, 1991.

SCENTLESS APPRENTICE

ALTHOUGH Pat Smear was credited as second guitarist on this performance, recorded (and filmed) for an MTV 'Live And Loud New Year's Special' at Pier 48, in Seattle, on December 13, 1993, he appeared to get lost amidst this overdose of magnificent power-trio riffing.

HEART-SHAPED BOX

THIS, THE last Nirvana single issued before Cobain's death, was greeted by a big cheer as soon as the opening guitar phrase tumbled out. The occasion was one of the band's final US shows, at the Great Western Forum, in Los Angeles, on the December 30, 1993. Once again, Pat Smear was on second guitar.

MILK IT

A FEW DAYS later, Nirvana were back in Seattle where it all started, playing a string of dates at the Center Arena. This particular show was recorded on the January 5, 1994, and this version of one of the highlights of In Utero vented the band's more uncompromising streak.

NEGATIVE CREEP

THIS TRACK was taken from the Hallowe'en 1991 show at the Paramount Theatre in Seattle, which had already been raided for the two live cuts on the 'Come As You Are' CD single. A significant performance in Nirvana's career, in that they left Seattle as great white hopes and returned with their records ripping up the charts, the show was also filmed, and must be ripe for a full release at a future date.

POLLY

THE BIG rock version," wrote Krist Novoselic in his sleeve-note. This came from the earliest show sourced for the album, taped at the Astoria Theatre in London, on the December 5, 1989. It was the final night of the band's European tour supporting Tad, and featured Chad Channing on drums.

BREED

"ALSO RECORDED at the Astoria, this early version of 'Breed' was still known as 'Imodium' at this stage.

TOURETTE'S

TOURETTE'S' wasn't one of the better songs on *In Utero*, and according to Novoselic, had been hanging around for years. That makes it a strange choice for inclusion here, especially when so much other good material was available from this August 30, 1992 Reading Festival performance, often regarded as one of the band's finest.

(Krist Novoselic was less scathing than his on-stage partner when it came to en-masse singalongs to Nirvana's music. Where 'Cobain would only have seen an undignified submersion of the individual, the bassist recalled the audience's chant along to 'Lithium' at the festival as "a very cool moment in the history of the band".)

BLEW

THE NIRVANA album catalogue closed just as it had opened, with a sandpaper-voiced version of 'Blew', taped at the Paradiso, Amsterdam, in November 1991.

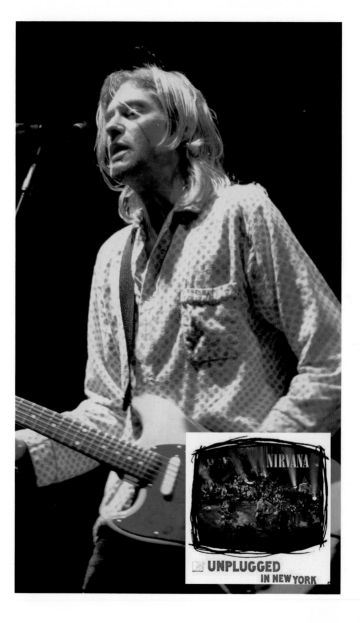

Nirvana Singles

6-CD box set, Geffen GED 24901, November 1995

THIS IS THE FIRST PORT OF CALL FOR NON-ALBUM TRACKS OTHER THAN THOSE already compiled onto *Incesticide*. Since Cobain's death, Geffen has been tightrope-walking between cashing in and dignified restraint regarding the lucrative Nirvana catalogue. This, simply the six CD singles lifted from the *Nevermind* and *In Utero* albums housed in a card box, was the first whiff of opportunism, a limited edition keepsake issued just in time for the Christmas rush. The pretext was that the less easily controlled German and Italian markets had already issued similar packages (as *The Nevermind & In Utero Singles* and *Grunge Is Dead* respectively), so why not protect the fan from hefty import prices? Spurious but true.

That said, ten non-album recordings (five studio, five live) were spread across the six singles, and if the UK edition of 'Lithium' had been used, a further studio out-take, 'D-7', would have been added to the list. But that would have negated the package's other selling-point – the inclusion of the complete lyrics to the *Nevermind* album, available only on the US edition of 'Lithium'. (In fact, all discs were replicas of the original US releases.)

Disc One

SMELLS LIKE TEEN SPIRIT (EDIT)

THIS WAS simply an edited version of the album track, trimmed by an inconsequential twenty seconds.

EVEN IN HIS YOUTH

A CLASSIC B-side in that it was distinctly second-rate Nirvana-by-numbers, prompting a real rarity – an uninspired performance from drummer Dave Grohl. You can probably put that down to shyness, because (radio sessions apart) this was his recording debut with the band.

The occasion was a New Year's Day 1991 session at Music Source, where the *Blew* EP had been recorded, but now with the band's full-time soundman Craig Montgomery at the controls. Even Cobain's concentration wasn't total, dropping a few words and turning in a guitar solo that, like the song's character, was "going nowhere". The self-loathing was still as potent as ever, though: "If I die, or crawl away, hope I don't come back the same".

ANEURYSM

THIS TOO was taped at the one-off Montgomery session, almost a year earlier than the recorded-for-radio version that ended up on *Incesticide*. There any real differences ended, because this is remarkably close to that album version, albeit given an added shot of adrenaline. Cobain later described this experimental session as "kind of screwy", and before release, remix engineer Andy Wallace performed a repair job on both tracks. This version first appeared on the *Hormoaning* import.

Disc Two

COME AS YOU ARE

SAME AS the album version (see *Nevermind*).

ENDLESS NAMELESS

FOR THOSE unlucky enough to have bought early copies of *Nevermind*, the six-and-a-half-minute-plus, all-instruments-blazing bonus jam provided a neat contrast to the airwave-friendly sound of the single.

SCHOOL (LIVE)
DRAIN YOU (LIVE)

THIS PAIR of non-album cuts were both recorded live at the Paramount Theatre, Seattle on Hallowe'en (October 31) 1991, a performance that has since been raided for a live CD and will no doubt yield more material in the future. The show was also filmed by Geffen, and the fact that nothing from it was used for the 'Live! Tonight! Sold Out!' video suggests that a full in-concert video/CD package is a strong possibility.

It was a good show to have documented, because it caught the band returning to their Seattle base in the immediate afterglow of *Nevermind*, which was still rising up the *Billboard* chart. Two days later, the album entered the Top 40, and the band set off to conquer Europe.

Disc Three

IN BLOOM

SAME AS the album version (see *Nevermind*).

SLIVER (LIVE)
POLLY (LIVE)

ANOTHER well-bootlegged Nirvana concert was the December 28, 1991 performance at the O'Brien Pavilion, Del Mar, California. Booked before 'Teen Spirit' and *Nevermind* transformed the band into the hottest ticket in town, this concert saw Nirvana playing the unhappy role of second support under Pearl Jam to The Red Hot Chili Peppers. Unhappier still, according to Azerrad's biography, these end-of-year dates marked the moment when bassist Krist Novoselic realised his on-stage partner was carrying a serious hero-in habit.

These two live recordings were more likely selected by name rather than performance: 'Sliver' was an old Sub Pop A-side that would be unknown to many of the band's new fans; 'Polly' was amplified, with subtle contributions from Novoselic and Grohl.

Disc Four

LITHIUM

SAME AS the album version (see *Nevermind*).

BEEN A SON (LIVE)

ANOTHER track raided from 1991's Hallowe'en show at the Paramount Theatre, Seattle, 'Been A Son' would have been familiar to the few thousand who bought the 'Blew' EP in 1989, but to no one else.

CURMUDGEON

THERE WAS something about the title (literally, "a surly or miserly person") that suggested Cobain wasn't wholly serious about this leftover from the first session with Butch Vig, taped in April 1990. Not to mention the burst of laughter that pre-empts the riff on which the song is based. With Vig's array of ancient equipment at his disposal, Cobain used the riff to build a heavily phased/flanged noisefest that owed more to mid-Seventies power trio Hot Tuna than it did to the Sex Pistols.

Disc Five

HEART-SHAPED BOX

SAME AS the album version (see *In Utero*).

MILK IT

SAME AS the album version (see *In Utero*).

MARIGOLD

THE ONLY song (excepting cover versions) in the entire Nirvana catalogue that didn't bear the mark of Kurt Cobain, 'Marigold' was the first indication that Dave Grohl had genuine songwriting aspirations. More than that, he also handled the lead vocals (which were as charming as Cobain's were tortured), and quite possibly the harmonies and the guitar too.

'Marigold' was subtle and brooding, its sparse sound echoing that of another Steve Albini-engineered band, the Breeders (fronted by ex-Pixie Kim Deal). In fact, it was a studio concoction, written at the *In Utero* sessions. Grohl revisited the song with his band Late, who included it on *Pocket Watch*, a cassette-only album issued on the US independent Simple Machines label.

Disc Six

ALL APOLOGIES

SAME AS the album version (see *In Utero*).

RAPE ME

SAME AS the album version (see *In Utero*).

MOIST VAGINA

ITS TALKING-point title, not to mention the amusing attempt to rhyme "vagina" with "marijuana", suggests that this, like 'Curmudgeon', was another hastily concocted studio jam. Maybe so, but what's essentially a bleak two-chord song was elevated by Cobain's oddly distressed celebration of two of the things that helped him forget pain and cynicism – sex and drugs.

'Moist Vagina', at one time modestly titled 'MV', was recorded at the *In Utero* sessions. Another leftover, 'Two Bass Kid', never made it onto an official release.

Nirvana

Geffen 493 523-2, October 2002

'You Know You're Right', 'About A Girl', 'Been A Son/Sliver', 'Smells Like Teen Spirit', 'Come As You Are', 'Lithium/In Bloom', 'Heart-Shaped Box', 'Pennyroyal Tea' (Scott Litt Mix), 'Rape Me/Dumb', 'All Apologies' (MTV *Unplugged* version), 'The Man Who Sold The World' (MTV *Unplugged* version), 'Where Did You Sleep Last Night' (MTV *Unplugged* version)

F OR YEARS, THE SUBJECT OF 'THE NIRVANA BOX SET', AN EXPANSIVE COLLECTION that would gather up all those hard-to-find songs recorded for compilations, elusive B-sides and – deep breath – never-before-heard gems from the Nirvana family archives, was an 'All in good time' topic. Hopes that it might be completed in time to celebrate the tenth anniversary of 'Smells Like Teen Spirit' were raised in October 1999, when Dave Grohl told BBC Radio 1: "The last song [Nirvana] ever recorded will be on there. That was from like February '94 or something. We went in to do a demo session and recorded one song, and not many people have heard it... maybe a handful of five or 10 people." That song was 'You Know You're Right', long rumoured to contain a lyric from the mixed-up mind of rock's finest post-punk icon. Grohl himself was even more excited about the material he'd not even played on. "I think the real jewels of that boxed set will be the really weird stuff that was recorded before I was in the band," he said.

Potential track-listings were drawn up and distributed among the inner circle, prompting whispers that this remarkable anthology of buried, grunge-era treasure would include more than 45 songs. Alongside a cache of Kurt's bedroom demos, recorded at various stages in his career, were live Nirvana recordings, including excerpts from the first show in Seattle in April 1988, four-track roughs, and embryonic versions of familiar songs. Apparently, there were around 120 tapes to sift through...

In May 2001, Courtney Love decided to extricate herself from previous agreements made with Grohl and Novoselic, as well as with Universal Music, and blocked the box. Kurt's ex-colleagues were incensed. "We were looking forward to releasing unheard Nirvana material for our personal sense of closure," they claimed in a self-styled 'Open Letter To Nirvana Fans'. "As the cycle of life moves forward, we are each living our own lives and moving on to new things. We only wanted to go on with the assurance of knowing that all of Nirvana's music is where it really belongs; in the hearts and minds of millions of people in the world." They also suggested that Love's move was prompted more by an "obsessive need for publicity and attention" than anything to do with the Nirvana legacy.

In a riposte from 'The Family Of Kurt Cobain', Love bit back. "Kurt Cobain was Nirvana. He named the band, hired its members, played guitar, wrote the songs, fronted the band onstage and in interviews and took responsibility for the band's business decisions. Kurt Cobain wrote almost all of Nirvana's music. Over 93% of the band's song copyrights are in his name."

The open letter continued: "Krist and Dave made an enormous musical contribution to Nirvana's success and they have been exceptionally well paid for that contribution and will continue to earn royalties from the catalogue's success... We look forward to many years of great releases from Kurt and Nirvana. We wish Krist and Dave great success in their current careers and hope they will soon leave control of Kurt's legacy to his rightful heirs."

The dirty business eventually found its way onto the cover of *Rolling Stone* magazine, in a piece titled 'Who Owns Kurt Cobain?' "It's just absolutely everything the band stood against and has nothing to do with why the band was a band in the first place," claimed an exasperated Dave Grohl. Most fans tended to agree with him. The Courtney Love-fronted Hole may have made one of the rock's finest albums in *Live Through This*, issued the week her husband died, and as his widow, no one doubts her claim to benefit from his legacy. But while there are rights, there are also wrongs, one of which is to let Kurt's legacy descend, Hendrix-like, into a disrespectful battle involving money, egos, anything, in fact, that threatens to overshadow the music and what it stands for.

The acrimony was sufficiently smoothed over for *Nirvana*, a predictable, remastered hits collection, spiced up by the inclusion of the spine-tingling 'You Know You're Right'. "I will never bother you/Never speak a word again/I will crawl away for good/I will move away from here... I always knew it would come to this," Cobain rasps, with eerie prescience.

It's far from certain whether this late January 1994 recording, one of the last tracks Cobain ever worked on, would have seen the light of day had it not been leaked on the internet a few months earlier. But Krist Novoselic was in no mood to complain: "I'm glad. If it were up to me, that song would have been out last year... It's a great performance by everybody and I'm glad that people get to hear it – finally."

Whether the peace can hold out long enough for what the bassist is now describing as an "encyclopaedic" Nirvana retrospective, tipped for release during 2004, is anyone's guess.

MISCELLANEOUS

Blew EP

Tupelo TUP CD 8, 1989

THE APPEARANCE ON *INCESTICIDE* OF BOTH NON-ALBUM TRACKS FROM THE 'Blew' EP masks the fact that the version of 'Been A Son' was a completely different take that had been recorded two years earlier. Like 'Stain', it was originally taped during the September 1989 'Blew' session at the Music Source Studio in Seattle. Producer Steve Fisk kept a tight rein on the rhythm section, but that aside, there isn't a great deal of difference between the two versions.

Sliver

Sub Pop SP 73; September 1990; vinyl only

THE ONLY WAY TO GET THE VERSION OF 'SLIVER' THAT FEATURES THE ANSWER- phone conversation between Krist Novoselic and Jonathan Poneman at the end of the song is by picking up the original single, which isn't as easy – or as cheap – as it sounds. This spoken-word oddity was removed from later Tupelo CD/12" repressings.

About A Girl (live)

Spank Thru (live)

Both Tupelo TUPCD 25, 1991

WHEN 'SLIVER' WAS REPRESSED, IT LOST A DISPENSABLE PHONE CONVERSATION and gained two live recordings, which are still unavailable anywhere else.

Molly's Lips (live)

Sub Pop 97, February 1991; vinyl only

ONCE AGAIN, *INCESTICIDE* SUBSTITUTED THE OFFICIALLY RELEASED TAKE WITH A radio session recording, ensuring that original copies of the 7,500-only Sub Pop Singles Club edition of The Vaselines' "Molly's Lips" are at a premium.

Cobain was hardly enthused by the release, later remarking that, "It was just a throwaway, a cover by one of our favourite UK bands. I like the song but the performance wasn't up to par." His lack of enthusiasm was deliberate: 'Molly's Lips' was Nirvana's final gift to Sub Pop, a contract-filler that became a shared single with the Denver-based band the Fluid, who contributed a live version of 'Candy'. In addition, Sub Pop received $70,000 compensation, a three per cent royalty and the label's logo on every future Nirvana release.

D-7

(Greg Sage)
Lithium CD single Geffen DGCSD 9, July 1992

THIS TRACK, ORIGINALLY RECORDED FOR THE BAND'S SECOND RADIO SESSION FOR John Peel, and subsequently compiled on the import-only *Hormoaning EP*, found the band celebrating veteran US punk band The Wipers. For some unspecified reason, it wasn't welcomed onto *Incesticide* to join the other three tracks taped that day.

Oh, The Guilt

Touch & Go TG 83 CD, February 1993

ANTICIPATION FOR THE FOLLOW-UP TO *NEVERMIND* WAS MET IN uncompromising fashion with this single, a shared disc with the Jesus Lizard (previously Cobain heroes Scratch Acid). Neither Butch Vig nor Andy Wallace were in sight for this tune-defying cut that was closer to the indus-trial-strength Big Black sound than to hard rock. As if to exorcise the demon of responsibility, and deflate the impossible expectations, the craftmanship of *Nevermind* was eschewed in favour of a form of rudimentary rage that made *Bleach* sound positively cuddly.

'Oh, The Guilt' (originally called 'It Takes A Time') was recorded in April

1992 at the Laundry Room studios, an occasional haunt of Dave Grohl who was crafting some of his own material with the aid of Barrett Jones, his drum-tech, pal and producer. Jones also oversaw this Nirvana session, which saw few of the production frills of the band's 1991 work. It was a luxury they could afford, for the single was a one-off for the Chicago-based Touch & Go label, coupled with the Jesus Lizard's 'Puss', and therefore tailored towards the specialist market – a smart move in order to rebuild credibility among those wary of Nirvana's corporate moves.

The 'Priest' They Called Him

(Kurt Cobain/William Burroughs)
Tim Kerr 92CD044, August 1993

AS IT TURNED OUT, 'OH, THE GUILT' WAS A REASONABLY ACCURATE PRIMER FOR *In Utero*. It's unlikely, though, that this collaboration with octogenarian Beat writer William Burroughs harboured many clues as to Cobain's musical direction in the final months of his life. In fact, it was recorded almost a year before its release, Burroughs taping his spoken-word monologue in September 1992, with Cobain adding his heavily-treated guitar sounds and feedback two months later.

Burroughs, whose famous comment that a paranoid was someone who knew exactly what was going on was echoed in Cobain's "Just because you're paranoid/Doesn't mean they're not after you" quip in 'Territorial Pissings', was living-proof that a lifetime's friendship with heroin, guns, misanthropy and misogyny, wasn't harmful. In fact, it had made him a legend far beyond Beat culture obsessives, with notable rock tie-ups with David Bowie in 1973 and Throbbing Gristle at the end of the Seventies. Watching Cobain linking hands with the wise old sage was like watching a burning torch being passed on in relay fashion.

'The 'Priest' They Called Him' was Burroughs' show, with Cobain's guitar howling nestling in the background, providing a disturbing ambience to the writer's dark-humoured Christmas street tale. The only real affinity between Burroughs' words and Cobain's backing music was the occasional intrusion of the melody of the Christmas carol, 'Silent Night'.

Bass-spotters might like to know that the chap dressed in the priestly gear for the cover photo was Krist Novoselic.

TRACKS ON COMPILATIONS

Spank Thru

(Sub Pop 200, Sub Pop SP 25, 1990)

ONE OF THE BAND'S EARLIEST TRACKS, 'SPANK THRU', WAS ORIGINALLY recorded at the January 23, 1988 Reciprocal session with engineer Jack Endino. The version that appeared on disc towards the end of that year was a re-recording featuring Chad Channing on drums, taped at the 'Love Buzz' session on June 11.

Despite its intriguing title, 'Spank Thru' was based on a three-chord-trick wildly reminiscent of Them's 'Gloria', took a while to kick in, and revealed Cobain to be a bit of a student of Led Zeppelin's Robert Plant in the vocal department. Anyone expecting a simple blend of R&B and soft metal might have been disappointed by the delightful punk rock atonality of the guitar break.

The track first appeared on a limited edition three-EP box set, titled *Sub Pop 200*, in December 1988, which was made more widely available many months later as a single CD.

Here She Comes Now

(Heaven And Hell Vol. 1 [A Tribute To The Velvet Underground] Imaginary Illusion 016 CD, 1990)

IT'S ONLY IN RETROSPECT THAT WE CAN SEE THAT ONE OF NIRVANA'S MOST important legacies was puncturing the enduring reverence for the Velvet Underground. Without a doubt one of the five most influential groups of all-time, the New York minimalists' legacy had become a curse by the early Eighties, when all manner of twee English bands knocked the stuffing out of the independent sector's boundary-breaking principle by falling back on the Velvets' third album for second-hand inspiration. Goodbye Prag Vec, hello *(yaaawn)* Postcard.

At least Nirvana's take on the band was less reverential. The omens weren't great to begin with, though, as the band played the 'White Light/White heat' album track straight, albeit with a ham-fist. Midway through, Cobain upped the ante, his larynx now loosened, and the song was extended into an approximation of a Cream workout, something neither Warhol nor Reed would ever have envisaged for their mixed-media band/project.

In Bloom

(Sub Pop Video Network Program One, Atavistic, 1990)

THE ORIGINAL SMART STUDIOS VERSION OF 'IN BLOOM', PRODUCED BY BUTCH Vig in April 1990, quietly crept onto the market on this various-artist video compilation.

Do You Love Me

(Paul Stanley, Kim Fowley & Bob Ezrin)
(Hard To Believe LP, Southern DAMP 121, 1991)

NIRVANA'S AMERICAN FANS MIGHT HAVE HAD NO PROBLEM WITH THEIR delight in grizzly Seventies US stadium rockers like Kiss, but British fans, to whom the gruesome foursome were Glam Rock with neither the fun nor the anthems, or hard rock without any real kick-ass, or – even worse – a pantomime act, would have found the track harder to stomach. Such are the peculiarities of transatlantic musical tastes.

Nirvana saw no shame in recording a storming version of Kiss's 'Do You Love Me', from their 1976 *Destroyer* album. It was taped in June 1989, during a session at Evergreen State College, Olympia (where an early version of 'Dive' was also recorded, as 'Down With Me'). A good home for this convivial take was found on C/Z's 'Hard To Believe' compilation, originally issued in the US in August 1990, and in the UK several months later.

Return Of The Rat

(Greg Sage)
(14 Songs For Greg Sage And The Wipers, Tim Kerr 91CD10, 1993)

THE WIPERS HAD ALREADY BEEN GIVEN THE NIRVANA SEAL OF APPROVAL WHEN 'D-7' was recorded for John Peel's Radio 1 show in 1990, and subsequently issued on the *Hormoaning* import. This second Wipers song was duly dusted down during a November 1991 session with Barrett Jones at the Laundry Room.

'Return Of The Rat' was more straight-ahead punk rock than 'D-7', and the sound of Cobain making no attempt to cover up his cough at the end of the first chorus emphasised the off-the-cuff nature of the performance. The track was first issued in June 1992 as part of the 'Eight Songs For Greg Sage And The Wipers' four-coloured-vinyl singles box set, which found its way onto a more manageable single CD edition a few months later.

Verse Chorus Verse

(No Alternative, Arista 07822 18737 2, 1993)

THE UNLISTED 19TH TRACK ON THIS AIDS BENEFIT COMPILATION ALBUM, 'Verse Chorus Verse' finally enshrined Cobain's popular dismissal of his band's music in song. Although an out-take from the *In Utero* sessions, there are elements on this track that suggest a clear affinity with Hole's layered-guitar style. What's the betting that the oft-repeated "Make you happy" line was a reference to Cobain's attempt to write a song for his new wife?

I Hate Myself And I Want To Die

(The Beavis And Butt-Head Experience, Geffen GED 24613, 1993/4)

THIS TRACK HAD BEEN AROUND SINCE 1990, ORIGINALLY AS A BUTCH VIG DEMO, when it was titled 'Sappy'. Like 'Verse, Chorus, Verse', this song might have been a potential title track for what became *In Utero*, though the likelihood is that it derived its title posthumously (as in post-*In Utero*, rather than post-Cobain).

Pay To Play

(DGC Rarities Volume One, Geffen, 1994)

THE ORIGINAL VERSION OF 'STAY AWAY', RECORDED AT SMART STUDIOS WITH Butch Vig in April 1990 crept out on this Geffen odds-and-sods compilation in 1994.

Radio Friendly Unit Shifter (Live)

(Home Alive, 2-CD, Epic 1996)

THIS ANTI-RAPE FUNDRAISER RECEIVED A SIGNIFICANT BOOST WITH THIS LIVE version of the *In Utero* track, which seemed to confirm that Nirvana songs will continue to creep out on compilations with progressive agendas attached.

Rape Me (Live)

Saturday Night Live: The Musical Performances Vol 2, Dreamwork 0044-50206-2, 1999

THIS COLLECTION OF LIVE SNL PERFORMANCES INCLUDES 'RAPE ME' AS performed live on the show by Nirvana on 25 September 1993.

INTERVIEW DISCS

Nevermind It's An Interview

Geffen PROCD 4382, 1991
US promo with four exclusive live cuts.

Nirvana

Sound And Media SAM 7008, 1995
Limited edition with 120-page book, card sleeve.

The Rockview Interviews

Rockview RVCD 201, 1996

The Bark Not The Bite

Gatefold digipak, DIST 003, 1996

A Tribute To Nirvana

Tribute TR 02

Telltales

Picture disc, Telltales TELL 07

The Unauthorised Biography
Of Kurt Cobain

Chrome Dreams ABCD 140, 2003

ONLY THE FIRST OF THESE WAS OFFICIALLY SANCTIONED; THE REST ARE CASH-INS released by opportunist companies aware that there are no copyright restrictions on spoken-word material.

Aside from *Nevermind It's An Interview*, which sells for daft money, the rest aren't really worth paying more than a fiver each for – and that's if you're really keen and willing to sit through plenty of waffle with the kind of journalist who later hands over his or her tapes for small financial gain. Several of these have been repackaged under different names. Approach this field with caution.

VIDEOS

The following two videos are well worth investigating.

Sonic Youth: 1991 – The Year Punk Broke

Geffen GEFV 39518, 1992

THIS HAND-HELD PIECE OF REPORTAGE BY DAVE MARKEY FOLLOWS SONIC Youth and their American pals on a European tour during 1991. Nirvana get a fair airing, with live versions of 'School', 'Endless, Nameless', 'Smells Like Teen Spirit' and 'Polly' sidling up alongside some typical on-tour antics (Cobain dancing with Kim Gordon, enjoying a shake'n'spray experience with a bottle of wine, meeting Courtney Love and headbutting a stack of amps). It's a great portrait of a scene on the cusp of a breakthrough, though Thurston Moore's amusing and obviously silly narrative seems to be regarded as pretension twaddle by many.

Live! Tonight! Sold Out!

With miniature booklet, Geffen GEFV 39541, 1994

THIS, THE BAND'S ONLY OFFICIAL FULL-LENGTH VIDEO, IS AN ESSENTIAL ADDITION to any Nirvana CD collection, its collage-like approach mirroring perfectly the band's explosive if short-lived contribution to rock culture.

Among the live performances included are: Aneurysm (Amsterdam, Holland, 1991; Sao Paulo, Brazil, 1993); About A Girl (Seattle, 1992); Dive (Sao Paulo, 1993); Love Buzz (Dallas, Texas, 1991; Amsterdam, 1991); Breed (Seattle, 1992); Smells Like Teen Spirit (*Top Of The Pops*, 1991; Amsterdam, 1991); Negative Creep (Honolulu, Hawaii, 1992); Come As You Are (Amsterdam, 1991); Territorial Pissings (*Jonathan Ross Show*, 1991; Amsterdam, 1991); Something In The Way (Tokyo, Japan, 1991); Lithium (Reading Festival, 1992); Drain You (Amsterdam, 1991); Polly (Seattle, 1992); Sliver (Amsterdam, 1991); On A Plain (Roskilde Festival, Denmark, 1992).

The following videos are unofficial and essentially superfluous:

Kurt Cobain: The Godfather Of Grunge

BS Video BS 11001, 1994

Kurt Cobain, Teen Spirit

Labyrinth LML 0266, 1995

Teen Spirit – The Tribute To Kurt Cobain

1995

FOO FIGHTERS

THERE WAS NEVER ANY SUGGESTION THAT NIRVANA COULD CONTINUE AFTER THE events of April 1994. Dave Grohl and Krist Novoselic, whose natural talent for mischief had helped temper Cobain's more troubled moments, were left seemingly high and dry. Imagine if Charlie Watts and Bill Wyman had been unceremoniously dumped by the rest of the Rolling Stones in 1966.

As the band's drummer, Dave Grohl probably had the most difficult job. History has not been kind to those who try to lead bands from the back, or who forsake the shadows for centre-stage. The Dave Clark Five and Ringo Starr may have sold millions of records in their time, but you'll be hard pushed to find a kind word on the durability of their work.

Unknown to most, Grohl's track-record had been good. He started out on guitar as a teenager, and that was the instrument he played with his first band, Freak Baby, in 1984. Four years later, while drumming with Washington DC's premier punk rock crew Scream, Grohl recorded several of his own songs, with old pal Barrett Jones handling the eight-track. Recalling the session in 1995, he said: "That summer, I realised that if I were to write a song, record the drums first, then come back over it with a few guitars, bass and vocals, I could make it sound like a band. So I came up with a few riffs on the spot and recorded three songs in under fifteen minutes. Mind you, these were no epic masterpieces, just a test to see if I could do this sort of thing on my own."

Even after Grohl was poached to join Nirvana, he maintained his working relationship with engineer Barrett Jones, whom he'd known since 1984. On occasion, he would also venture elsewhere to record his growing repertoire of songs. Once *Nevermind* was in the bag, for example, he returned home to Washington DC for a few days, and worked on material at a different studio. These songs were heard by Jenny Toomey of the independent Simple Machines label, who promptly released them as the cassette-only *Pocketwatch* album, under the alter-ego Late. Among the songs were early versions of 'Marigold' (later a Nirvana B-side) and 'Winnebago'.

While busy in the wake of the success of *Nevermind*, Grohl continued to write his own material on tour, which he'd then record once he was back in Seattle. By this time, Barrett Jones had moved to Seattle, and the pair had established their own eight-track basement studio. After touring Europe and America, Grohl and Jones got to work, recording a dozen or so of Grohl's songs during this period. Another quiet spell for Nirvana during the summer of 1992 enabled Grohl to experiment further with harmonies and arrangements. When 'Marigold' appeared as a Nirvana B-side, in 1993, it seemed as if the drummer might be able to carve out a more sizeable role for himself within the group. Cobain's death put an abrupt halt to that.

Foo Fighters

Roswell/Capitol 7243 8 340272 June 4, 1995

IN THE AFTERMATH OF **KURT COBAIN'S** DEATH, **DAVE GROHL** RECEIVED A MESSAGE of support from Seattle band 7 Year Bitch, who'd also lost a band member through tragic circumstances. It was the tonic he needed. "That fucking letter saved my life," he later admitted. Inspired into action, he "decided to do what I had always wanted to do since the first time I'd recorded a song all by myself. I was going to book a week in a 24-track studio, choose the best stuff I'd ever written out of the 30-40 songs that had piled up, and really concentrate on them in a real studio."

The sessions, which took place at Robert Lang's Studio, Seattle, between October 17 and 24, 1994, were co-produced by Grohl and his longtime associate Barrett Jones. Grohl: "He was the only person in the world I felt comfortable singing in front of. Over the past six years, Barrett and I had perfected our own method of recording: start with the drums, listen to the playback while humming the tune in my head to make sure the arrangement is correct, put down two or three guitar tracks... saving the vocals for last."

Within a week, Grohl's new record was already at the rough mix stage. He had no band, nor even a name for the project, but he did have the raw material for an album that seemed likely to guarantee him a post-Nirvana career.

After fruitless jams with several hopefuls, the singing sticks-man met Sunny Day Real Estate bassist Nate Mendel through their respective girlfriends. Extremely popular in Seattle, and with one Sub Pop album to their name, the band were on the verge of breaking up by the end of a midsummer 1994 tour. "I saw them play their last few shows in Seattle and was blown away by Nate and Will (drummer William Goldsmith)," Grohl remembered. "So you can imagine my first reaction when I heard the band was calling it quits. I gave the two of them tapes through my wife's friend and prayed they'd enjoy them."

Another early recipient of Grohl's tape was Pat Smear, the ex-Germs guitarist who'd become a fourth member of Nirvana in its final months. "After you've been in the coolest band ever, what do you do?" he later asked. Smear's rehabilitation began by spending the best part of a year in front of the television with a remote control in his hand. "I didn't even know if I ever wanted to be in a band again," he said. "I was just working on solo stuff. Dave and I had kept in touch, and when I heard his tape, I flipped."

By now working as Foo Fighters, Grohl's new band debuted in Seattle in March 1995, the month which also saw Grohl finishing work on his album. The name derived from American war-time pilots who claimed to see UFOs in the skies above Germany. Some believed these to be a new enemy weapon called "Kraut balls". Maintaining the military-and-aliens theme, Grohl signed a deal for the album with Capitol, who would release the record in conjunction with his own Roswell label, named after the American Air Force base where an alien was supposedly captured and photographed in 1947.

As news came in that the Foo Fighters' debut album was imminent, the joke was that Dave Grohl was about to become 'Grunge Ringo'. (This ignores the fact that during his 1971-73 peak, the ex-Beatles' drummer was selling more singles than either John Lennon or Paul McCartney.) People had come to scoff, though such low expectations invariably worked in Grohl's favour: right across the board, *Foo Fighters* was a critical success without ever having to rely on the sympathy vote. That success was reflected commercially, with the album, and the singles taken from it, transforming Foo Fighters into a major international name. A studio-based Nirvana follow-up might have had trouble equalling the Foo's' success.

Foo Fighters was grunge-lite. It was power-pop in the tradition of the Raspberries, Big Star and The Lemonheads. It was melodic like The Beatles and The Beach Boys, with the bark of The Pixies, Hüsker Dü and, yes, Nirvana. It was the winning smile that hid no anguish. It was a perfect antidote to recent events, and at a stroke, the record seemed to purge Grohl of the weight of historical burden.

Four of the songs, 'Alone + Easy Target', 'Floaty', 'Good Grief' and 'Exhausted', had been originally demoed by Grohl during the summer 1991 stint with Barrett Jones, just before *Nevermind* broke. Even at this early stage, it was clear that Grohl's songs wore an altogether friendlier face that those of his mother band. By 1995, only 'Alone + Easy Target' bore much relation to Nirvana, and then via its title as much as anything else. (The decision to illustrate a handgun on the front cover was the most blatant attempt to engineer a talking-point in this respect.)

The most extraordinary revelation on the Foo Fighters début was Grohl's voice, a nasal whine with a range capable of reaching those elusive high notes. It was a perfect pop front for songs that bounced effortlessly away from the Nirvana style, which had alternated moodily from slouch to sprint.

The debut 45, 'This Is A Call', typified this transition. Its subject matter consisted of fingernails, medicines, molluscs, magic-markers and balloons; and Grohl's delivery sounded uncannily like Neil Young with a rocket up his bottom. As with all Foo Fighters singles, the B-side included non-album tracks, on this occasion 'Winnebago' and 'Podunk'. The second, 'I'll Stick Around', included 'How I Miss You' and 'Ozone'; 'For All The Cows' was backed by live versions of the A-side and 'Wattershed' while the hitherto unissued 'Gas Chamber' turned up on the flip of 'Big Me'. A live version of 'This Is A Call', taped in June 1996, subsequently turned up on the *Tibetan Freedom Concert* 3-CD compilation.

The Colour
And The Shape

Parlophone 7243 8 55832 2 3, May 1997

FOO FIGHTERS HAD EXCEEDED EVERYONE'S EXPECTATIONS. HOWEVER, BY March 1997, Dave Grohl was giving it a wide berth, telling *Melody Maker* that it was like "a glorified demo tape. I went down to a studio, recorded it in five days, didn't spend much time or energy on it, took it for what it was and thought, 'That sounds kind of cool'." Having spent the past two years working full-time with a band, he was quick to make light of his multi-instrumental abilities. "I don't know how to fuckin' play the bass! I think I was just following the guitar!" Grohl, the man who once said, "All I wanted to do was be Keith Moon, with the kick-drum foot of John Bonham," had become a fully-fledged front-man, songwriter and artiste.

He was also a proud bandleader, happy to tell journalists that *The Colour And The Shape* was really the Foo Fighters' first album. "It's all of us together recording," he told *Melody Maker*, "and the songwriting process was entirely different. I'd come in with an idea and everyone would take it in their own direction." That it boasted a bigger sound than the debut album was less to do with the new producer, Gil Norton (famed for his work with The Pixies), and more with the new spirit of collaboration. Pat Smear's guitar playing was quite different to Grohl's own; Nate was a proper bassist; and William Goldsmith, who drummed on the album but had quit shortly before its release, also had his own style.

Grohl had also taken his songwriting to new levels. "It's the first time I've had the confidence as a songwriter to really get into the lyrics," he told *NME*, adding that the record was "all about everything that's happened to me in the last 18 months".

Despite all that, *The Colour And The Shape* was still recognisably the follow-up to the 1995 album, on which no other musician (other than Greg Dulli, who played guitar on 'X-Static') had played a note. The group, now with three bearded members, looked different. Grohl had even got himself a haircut. And there was new drummer Taylor Hawkins, poached from Alanis Morissette's backing band. But increased sophistication hadn't altered the band's basic musical outlook. The first single, 'Monkey Wrench', was hi-energy power-pop of the first order. 'Wind Up' was punkish metal; 'Up In Arms' punkish pop; and 'Walking After You' rock balladry of an almost traditional kind. Meanwhile, the opening 'Doll' could have been an out-take from a solo album by the late Beach Boy Dennis Wilson.

Then there was 'My Hero'. Back in 1995, Grohl insisted that, "None of our songs are about Kurt. I wouldn't do that to him. I wouldn't embarrass him like that." Two years later, the little man in the moth-eaten green cardigan and faded blue jeans who used to dart about in front of Grohl's kit, had made his first visitation to a Foo Fighters song. Grohl explained that the track was "about having friends you consider your hero and they're just ordinary people... There's definitely an element of Kurt in that song. It was probably inspired by him. That was probably my realisation that these people who are normal human beings can be way more than a famous figure."

More non-album material slipped out across the many B-sides. Various editions of 'Monkey Wrench' included a version of Tubeway Army's 'Down In The Park', a slow 'Up In Arms', an acoustic 'See You' and the album's missing title track, 'The Colour And The Shape'. A cover of Killing Joke's 'Requiem', live versions of 'I'll Stick Around' and 'See You', plus a cover of Vanity 66's 'Drive Me Wild' joined the permutations of 'Everlong. 'My Hero' was bolstered by 'Dear Lover', an acoustic 'For All The Cows' and a cover of Gerry Rafferty's annoying Seventies hit, 'Baker Street', while 'Walking After You' was remixed for single release. A French Inedits issue of the album added live versions of 'Winnebago' and 'Weenie Beenie' recorded in France.

There Is Nothing Left To Lose

RCA/Roswell 74321 71699 2, November 1999

THE TEMPLATE ESTABLISHED BY THE FOOS ACROSS THE FIRST TWO ALBUMS WAS evident once again on album #3, though the more relaxed vibe in the studio was countered by more fractious events outside. First, guitarist Pat Smear had quit by the time *The Colour And The Shape* was released. His replacement, ex-Scream Franz Stahl, didn't last long, either. That left a nucleus of Grohl, bassist Nate Mendel and drummer Taylor Hawkes to work on the album.

Eschewing Gil Norton's multiple takes approach that characterised the making of the previous record, the trio retreated to Grohl's Studio 606 in Virginia with producer Adam Kasper, plugged into their AC30s – the combo favoured by Sixties garage bands – and cranked up the volume. "We focused on not using too many distortion pedals, and went for a cleaner, fatter, more natural overdrive," insisted Grohl, who'd killed time between albums by recording the soundtrack to Paul Schrader's 'Touch'.

Selecting takes based on feel, and to hell with the imperfections, suited The Foo Fighters' relaxed, enthusiastic approach well. "Everyone was afraid we'd go and make a *White Album* or some freaky Einsturzende Neubauten record or something," Grohl told *Melody Maker*. "I was talking to my manager on the phone and he goes, 'You know what I need, Dave? I need 12 singles.'"

Well, he got four – 'Learn To Fly', 'Generator', 'Breakout' and 'Next Year' – all of which maintained the Foos' respectable singles chart profile, and put a successful seal on the band's new relationship with RCA/BMG. The same combination of hook-laden rock songs and raucous, good-natured angst continued to loosen the ties with Grohl's past, while a succession of wacky videos helped raise his profile from plucky drummer to cheeky frontman with a fast-growing female following. Less endeared of him, though, was Kurt Cobain's widow Courtney Love, who regarded the opening 'Stacked Actors' (which references bountiful breasts, dead blondes and ageing drag queens) as a thinly veiled attack on her.

Grohl wasn't unduly concerned. The Foo Fighters had at last emerged from the shadows of his past, touring the world's arenas and threatening to become the new Queen. The second guitarist problem had finally been solved by the recruitment of ex-No Use For A Name's Chris Shiflett. And Grohl – the self styled "loser redneck from Virginia" – was having the time of his life, sending out anti-homophobic messages via a series of photo shoots and video promos that had him decked out in women's clothing. "It takes a big man to wear a dress," he said, echoing sentiments uttered by Cobain several years earlier. "It was important to Nirvana, it was important to us, it's important to me."

Bonus material generously heaped across the 45s this time round included 'Make A Bet' and covers of Pink Floyd's 'Have A Cigar' and the Obsessed's 'Iron And Stone' (on 'Learn To Fly'); live versions of 'Ain't It The Life', 'Floaty' and 'Breakout' (on 'Generator'); 'Learn To Fly', 'Stacked Actors', 'Monkey Wrench' and 'Next Year' all taped live in Sydney (on 'Breakout'); and live versions of 'Big Me' and 'Next Year' (on Next Year').

One By One

BMG/Roswell 74321 71699-2, October 2002

FOR A WHILE, THE FOO FIGHTERS LOOKED LIKE SUCCUMBING TO THAT AGE-OLD 'victims of their own success' syndrome. The virtually continuous world tour on the back of *There Is Nothing Left To Lose*, took the band well into 2001, after which they seemed to disappear up four separate avenues.

Dave Grohl kept himself busy with numerous cameo roles, joining in sessions for David Bowie, Tenacious D, Probot and, most notably, Queens Of The Stone Age – anyone, it seemed, bar the Foo Fighters. As if Grohl's new, nomad-like existence wasn't enough, the Foos' premier party animal drummer Taylor Hawkins collapsed in London one night in August 2001. A victim of rock excess, certainly, but it can't be easy drumming for a band fronted by arguably the finest rock'n'roll drummer in the world.

Hawkins snapped out of a coma after two days, and this episode – since referred to as "Taylor's nap" in Foo-lore – seemed to spur the band into action. Regrouping in Grohl's Virginia studio, they worked up several songs, then booked into a hi-tech studio in LA to refine the material – and promptly lost the plot. "Far too clean, too tame and boring," was Grohl's verdict on these 'million-dollar demos'. The pressure of writing another set of hit singles also proved intimidating, so he went out on the road with Queens Of The Stone Age, and bashed hell out of his old kit instead. The rest of the band – and management and fans – had begun to write off the possibility of there ever being a fourth Foo Fighters album.

The resulting *One By One* remains a testament to the rejuvenating effect of Grohl's 'busman's holiday'. Just twelve days locked up in his Studio 606, working up what he later admitted were "11 tortured love songs", on guitar, drums and scratch bass, produced the basis of finest Foo Fighters set yet. "We went back and re-recorded everything, re-recorded any song we wanted to, and wrote couple more," said Hawkins. "It was our manager who told us, 'Just fucking go for it, just do whatever.'" After a little finessing in a posh California studio, the Foo Fighters had a new album in the bag in the space of three weeks.

"This album is the best we've ever made," Grohl told Sasha Stojanovic. It wasn't simply hype. "I can't wait to do more interviews, you know. I'm excited to talk about the album. Before, I couldn't give a shit; just give someone a fucking CD and tell them to go and figure it out... I am so proud of it."

Dynamics is the word that immediately springs to mind as opening 'All My Life' breathes, then bursts into life. Its teeth-grinding edginess set the tone for the album, and it was obvious that Grohl's stint with Queens Of

The Stone Age had stirred up some raw bile to augment the sense of melody that comes naturally to him. The warring guitars and lackadaisical, stoner-like vocals of 'Low' were even more impressive, while the plaintive 'Tired Of You' proved that Grohl was still capable of a little gentle heart-tugging, aided by some subtle six-string decoration from Queen's Brian May.

As is the norm with Foo Fighters singles, 'All My Life', 'Times Like These' and 'Low' feature a range of non-LP bonus tracks. Notable titles to look out for include the Norwegian edition of the album, which includes a bonus disc containing four songs recorded live in Oslo (a fifth title, 'Snoof', is actually Dave Grohl grappling with the local language; 'Danny Says', 'The One', 'Win Or Lose' and 'Sister Europe' (on 'All My Life'); 'Normal', a cover of Joe Walsh's 'Life Of Illusion' and live versions of 'Learn To Fly' and the B-52's' 'Planet Claire' (on 'Times Like These'); live versions of 'Never Talking To You Again' and 'Enough Space', plus the video of 'Low' (on 'Low').

Some editions of the CD album also includes a bonus DVD element that includes the 'All My Life' video plus live footage. More recently, the band has issued a full-length DVD, *Everywhere But Home*, which includes nearly three hours of footage shot during their 2002/2003 world tour. After that comes Grohl's three-years-in-the-making Probox project, a multi-artist metal collaboration that boasts a lengthy list of guests – including Motorhead's Lemmy and a host of Eighties US underground rock frontmen. Meanwhile, the Foo Fighters look set to confound expectations much further with their next record, which they're already calling their version of The Beatles' *White Album*...

KRIST NOVOSELIC

DAVE GROHL'S REMARKABLE VAULT OVER HIS KIT AND INTO THE INTERNATIONAL rock mainstream was as unlikely as it was unprecedented. Back in the dark days of 1994, the smart money was on Nirvana bassist Krist Novoselic re-emerging, bruised but nevertheless battled-hardened enough to pick up from where the band left off. One surprisingly anonymous decade later, Novoselic finally seems poised to break out – albeit in a surprisingly different guise.

Neither Sweet 75 or Eyes Adrift, the two bands he's formed since 1994, made much impression either on old Nirvana fans or new audiences. The lanky bassman, whose brilliant 'Get Together' parody at the start of 'Territorial Pissings' remains a prime Nirvana moment, was in danger of being forgotten. But in many ways he shared Kurt Cobain's misgivings about the fame game, and his subsequent low-key musical endeavours bear that out. But Novoselic also shared his fallen comrade's antipathy to the iniquities of American 'democracy', so it's no surprise that the ex-Nirvana bassist appears destined to take his – and the band's – ideals into the political arena.

Speaking at a political convention at Portland University in November 2003, he declared: "Nirvana's political passions were bred in the punk rock and hardcore music scene of the 1980s. This scene wasn't just about fresh music. It was supported by the ideals of fairness and freedom. We really cared about equality, human rights and American foreign policy, among other issues. Fairness and freedom were a big part of the music and counterculture of those times."

Acknowledging that success inevitably sucked the band into the mainstream, he nevertheless claimed that "We brought our honest ideals with us. I look back at 1991 as not only a musical movement; there was also a cultural shift... Nirvana was a political band. We were the prophets of the disenfranchised. We spoke to the disenfranchised because we ourselves felt that way."

By August 1997, and with Grohl's Foo Fighters already on their second successful album, Novoselic must have been feeling especially disenfranchised. *Sweet 75*, the band he'd formed with Yva Las Vegas, a feisty singer from Venezuela, released their self-titled debut (Geffen DGC 25140) to a loud-sounding silence. Not that anonymity would have entirely displeased him, because Sweet 75 was a laid-back affair that was anything but Nirvana – The Sequel. "We were especially conscious of breaking out of the traditional rock album mold," Novoselic commented at the time. "We have a horn section on a few songs ('La Vida', which featured Easy Listening trumpet legend Herb Alpert, 'Dogs'), and we also included a traditional

Venezuelan folk song ('Cantos de Pilon', with R.E.M.'s Peter Buck making a cameo on mandolin)."

Ominously, Novoselic, who'd swapped his bass for an electric 12-string guitar (Yva sang and played bass, Adam Wade drummed) claimed: "We're not The Monkees. We don't have an identity or a gimmick. We're a real band." But reality was no substitute for sales and the group, whose name derived from a Roethke poem, remained an exotic plaything that by the end of the decade had lost its novelty value.

Within a year, Novoselic was back on familiar territory: on bass and trading licks with Curt Kirkwood, the ex-Meat Puppets guitarist who famously joined Nirvana for the *Unplugged In New York* show. With ex-Sublime drummer Bud Gaugh, this new trio, Eyes Adrift, was a self-styled "tragedy all-star" band, due to the fact that each member had lost a close musical friend.

The rootsy Americana of Eyes Adrift's self-titled September 2002 debut (Spin Art SPART 115) was fashionable and, maintained the bassist, blessed by Kurt from the other side, but still Novoselic – who sang a bit and wrote a handful of songs – remained disenfranchised. "We're pros, and we're just glad to have an audience come out and see us," he enthused to one writer at the end of one interview. His optimism didn't last. By the following summer, news trickled out that Eyes Adrift were no more, and that Novoselic was giving up music. It wasn't quite true: "I haven't quit music; I've just quit the business," he countered.

Within months, he announced that he was seriously considering running for the post of Lieutenant Governor in the 2004 Washington State elections. He's nailed his mast to the Democratic Party, but judging by several years of active politics (he founded JAMPAC – the Joint Artists and Music Promotions Political Action Committee – back in the mid-Nineties to campaign on behalf of the local music community), Novoselic, won't be afraid to speak his mind. An advocate of proportional representation, which he feels will mobilise the huge rump of disenfranchised communities in the world's most disinterested democracy, he may just have found his forte.

Index